An Analysis of

Robert A. Dahl's

Democracy and Its Critics

Astrid Norén-Nilsson
with
Elizabeth Morrow and Riley Quinn

Published by Macat International Ltd
24:13 Coda Centre, 189 Munster Road, London SW6 6AW.

Distributed exclusively by Routledge
2 Park Square, Milton Park, Abingdon, Oxon OX14 4RN
711 Third Avenue, New York, NY 10017, USA

Routledge is an imprint of the Taylor & Francis Group, an informa business

www.macat.com
info@macat.com

Cataloguing in Publication Data
A catalogue record for this book is available from the British Library.
Library of Congress Cataloguing-in-Publication Data is available upon request.
Cover illustration: Etienne Gilfillan

ISBN 978-1-912303-22-9 (hardback)
ISBN 978-1-912127-34-4 (paperback)
ISBN 978-1-912282-10-4 (e-book)

CONTENTS

THE MACAT LIBRARY

The Macat Library is a series of unique academic explorations of seminal works in the humanities and social sciences – books and papers that have had a significant and widely recognised impact on their disciplines. It has been created to serve as much more than just a summary of what lies between the covers of a great book. It illuminates and explores the influences on, ideas of, and impact of that book. Our goal is to offer a learning resource that encourages critical thinking and fosters a better, deeper understanding of important ideas.

Each publication is divided into three Sections: Influences, Ideas, and Impact. Each Section has four Modules. These explore every important facet of the work, and the responses to it.

This Section-Module structure makes a Macat Library book easy to use, but it has another important feature. Because each Macat book is written to the same format, it is possible (and encouraged!) to cross-reference multiple Macat books along the same lines of inquiry or research. This allows the reader to open up interesting interdisciplinary pathways.

To further aid your reading, lists of glossary terms and people mentioned are included at the end of this book (these are indicated by an asterisk [*] throughout) – as well as a list of works cited.

Macat has worked with the University of Cambridge to identify the elements of critical thinking and understand the ways in which six different skills combine to enable effective thinking.
Three allow us to fully understand a problem; three more give us the tools to solve it. Together, these six skills make up the **PACIER** model of critical thinking. They are:

ANALYSIS – understanding how an argument is built
EVALUATION – exploring the strengths and weaknesses of an argument
INTERPRETATION – understanding issues of meaning

CREATIVE THINKING – coming up with new ideas and fresh connections
PROBLEM-SOLVING – producing strong solutions
REASONING – creating strong arguments

To find out more, visit **WWW.MACAT.COM.**

CRITICAL THINKING AND *DEMOCRACY AND ITS CRITICS*

Primary critical thinking skill: ANALYSIS
Secondary critical thinking skill: EVALUATION

There are few better examples of analysis – the critical thinking skill of understanding how an argument is built – than Robert Dahl's *Democracy and its Critics*. In this work, the American political theorist closely analyzes the democratic political system and then evaluates whether the arguments that are in favor of it are, in fact, rigorous.

Dahl sets out to describe democracy's merits and problems, asking if it really is the worthwhile political system we believe it to be. Knowing that the idea of democracy is now almost universally popular, his detailed analysis leads him to look at a number of regimes that claim to be democratic but do not, in truth, practice democracy. But Dahl is not only interested in uncovering uncomfortable truths. He goes further and creates a set of standards by which we can all decide whether a country really is democratic. Dahl's analysis of the evidence leads him to conclude that the following criteria must be met for a regime to be considered truly democratic: elected officials control policy-making; there are free and fair elections of officials; everyone must have a right to vote; everyone has the right to run for office; there is freedom of speech; alternative information is available; and people can form free, independent political groups.

ABOUT THE AUTHOR OF THE ORIGINAL WORK

Robert A. Dahl was born in 1915 in Iowa in the United States. He received his PhD in political science from Yale University in 1940, and after serving in the US Army during World War II, returned to Yale to become a professor, spending his entire academic career there. Over the next 40 years, he wrote prolifically, and many of his works, including *Who Governs? Democracy and Power in an American City* (1961), became key texts in the field of political science. Dahl also won a number of prestigious awards and helped Yale's department of political science become one of the most respected in the country. He died in 2014 at the age of 98.

ABOUT THE AUTHOR OF THE ANALYSIS

Dr Astrid Norén Nilsson holds a doctorate in politics and international studies from the University of Cambridge. She currently teaches at the University of Lund in Sweden, and is the author of the monograph *Cambodia's Second Kingdom: Nation, Imagination, and Democracy*. Her research interests include democratic change, nationalism, the politics of memory, and emerging notions of citizenship and social change in South-East Asia.

Dr Lindsay Scorgie Porter is visiting assistant professor in politics at the University of Western Ontario. She holds a PhD in politics and international studies from the University of Cambridge and an MSc in global politics from the London School of Economics.

Riley Quinn holds master's degrees in politics and international relations from both LSE and the University of Oxford.

ABOUT MACAT

GREAT WORKS FOR CRITICAL THINKING

Macat is focused on making the ideas of the world's great thinkers accessible and comprehensible to everybody, everywhere, in ways that promote the development of enhanced critical thinking skills.

It works with leading academics from the world's top universities to produce new analyses that focus on the ideas and the impact of the most influential works ever written across a wide variety of academic disciplines. Each of the works that sit at the heart of its growing library is an enduring example of great thinking. But by setting them in context – and looking at the influences that shaped their authors, as well as the responses they provoked – Macat encourages readers to look at these classics and game-changers with fresh eyes. Readers learn to think, engage and challenge their ideas, rather than simply accepting them.

'Macat offers an amazing first-of-its-kind tool for interdisciplinary learning and research. Its focus on works that transformed their disciplines and its rigorous approach, drawing on the world's leading experts and educational institutions, opens up a world-class education to anyone.'

Andreas Schleicher
Director for Education and Skills, Organisation for Economic Co-operation and Development

'Macat is taking on some of the major challenges in university education ... They have drawn together a strong team of active academics who are producing teaching materials that are novel in the breadth of their approach.'

Prof Lord Broers,
former Vice-Chancellor of the University of Cambridge

'The Macat vision is exceptionally exciting. It focuses upon new modes of learning which analyse and explain seminal texts which have profoundly influenced world thinking and so social and economic development. It promotes the kind of critical thinking which is essential for any society and economy. This is the learning of the future.'

Rt Hon Charles Clarke, former UK Secretary of State for Education

'The Macat analyses provide immediate access to the critical conversation surrounding the books that have shaped their respective discipline, which will make them an invaluable resource to all of those, students and teachers, working in the field.'

Professor William Tronzo, University of California at San Diego

WAYS IN TO THE TEXT

KEY POINTS

- Robert A. Dahl was an influential American political scientist who shaped the contemporary study of the system of government of democracy* and the mechanisms that define it, such as mass voting and the rule of law.

- Dahl's *Democracy and its Critics* considers the questions of what democracy is, and whether it is a desirable system of government.

- The book is important because it proposes a theoretical and practical definition of democracy that can be applied in many situations.

Who Was Robert A. Dahl?

Robert A. Dahl, the author of *Democracy and its Critics* (1989), was one of the most important political scientists of the twentieth century. His work, the result of a career spanning more than five decades, has transformed the contemporary understanding of democracy.

Dahl was born in Iowa in 1915, and grew up in a small town in the state of Alaska. He earned a PhD in political science at Yale University in 1940, where would spend the rest of his career. Appointed Eugene Meyer Professor of Political Science in 1955 and Sterling Professor of Political Science in 1964, he played an important role in building the reputation of the university's political science department as a world leader in the study of democracy. He died in 2014 at the age of 98.

Dahl said his interest in studying democracy started with his experience of growing up in a small town in Alaska. From the age of 12, he spent his summers working on the docks with longshore workers,* loading and unloading ships. This, together with his military service and his early experience of small town life, gave him a deep respect for what he called "plain ordinary human beings" and their common sense and abilities. These experiences taught him the importance of information and education in helping people protect their own self-interest, in turn inspiring him to work at describing modern democracy; his object was to study the real extent of democratization in the world.

What Does *Democracy and Its Critics* Say?

At its core, Dahl's *Democracy and Its Critics* asks what democracy means. A concept frequently taken for granted, Dahl set out to describe its merits and problems, asking if democracy is the worthwhile political system we believe it to be. The book was published during a period of major democratic transformation—a process that soon would accelerate with the collapse of the Soviet Union* in 1991, a nation whose political system, communism,* operated on notably undemocratic lines.

The question of what democracy means is of great importance, as many consider it to be the most desirable political system that exists. Democracy focuses on individual freedom and protection from abuse at the hands of the state. But democracy is not perfect. Some so-called democracies do not genuinely respect individual freedom, and serve merely as a cloak for non-democracy. Although the Egyptian government of Abdel Fattah el-Sisi* describes itself as democratic, for example, Sisi had only a single opponent in the 2014 election after disqualifying several others, and won with 93 percent of the vote— arguably an impossibly high margin.[1]

Some argue that nondemocratic forms of government may be superior to democracy; a state might make stability a higher priority than individual freedom, for example, which might help create economic growth and better living standards. The book focuses on what democracy is, and how it can be justified.

Dahl starts by explaining why democracy is desirable, and what its limits and possibilities are. He believes democracy is justified by its most basic democratic principle: that the interests of each person in a political community must be given equal consideration.* Dahl also examines criticism of democracy and problems in the democratic process. Finally, having developed a theory* of democracy and put forward a justification for it, Dahl offers suggestions for how polyarchies*—modern countries that have achieved some features of democracy yet fall short of democratic ideals—may draw closer to democracy. The standards Dahl proposes for a country to qualify as a polyarchy are:

- Elected officials control policy-making
- Free and fair elections of officials
- Inclusive suffrage,* meaning nearly everyone has a right to vote
- Everyone has the right to run for office
- Freedom of speech
- Alternative information is available
- People can form political groups that have autonomy*—the freedom to act independently.

According to Google Scholar, *Democracy and Its Critics* has been cited more than 7,000 times in scholarly publications, and there is little question that the book has had a huge influence on later scholarship; scholars have, for example, sought to develop Dahl's definition of polyarchy into a way of measuring how well political systems meet the minimum requirements for democracy.[2]

The global economic recession* that followed the financial crisis of 2007–8, meanwhile, offers an opportunity for further scholarship on Dahl's idea of democratic governance of private enterprise.

Why Does *Democracy and Its Critics* Matter?

Democracy and Its Critics is useful both for students of politics and for the nonacademic world of economics, finance, and business.

Dahl wanted *Democracy and Its Critics* to explain democracy completely.[3] Acknowledging that while the idea of democracy is almost universally popular but some regimes around the world that claim to be "democratic" do not actually practice democracy,[4] Dahl set out to create a set of standards to determine whether countries are democracies. Any government process that meets these standards entirely would be a perfect democratic process, and its government would be fully democratic.[5]

Democracy and Its Critics has become a modern classic in democratic theory, expanding on Dahl's large body of work on the topic in previous decades.[6] Dahl suggested creating bodies of randomly selected citizens who would deliberate on a particular policy issue, and the debate would bring back the face-to-face deliberation that characterized ancient democracy. He called such a body a "minipopulus";* although the term means "small group," Dahl proposed bodies as large as a thousand people. The idea of minipopuli has been important to theorists who aim to increase democratic deliberation and has been found useful by those analyzing problems of democracy such as declining turnout at elections.

Dahl's text is also important for business and economics; in it, he argues that economic structures should be regulated to ensure political equality, proposes work-place democracy, and reasons that the same democratic processes used in a nation-state should govern economic enterprises.[7]

NOTES

1 "Egypt election: Sisi secures landslide win," *BBC News*, May 29, 2014, accessed September 8, 2015, http://www.bbc.com/news/world-middle-east-27614776.

2 Michael Coppedge and Wolfgang H. Reinicke, "Measuring Polyarchy," *Studies in Comparative International Development* 25, no. 1 (1990): 51–72.

3 Robert A. Dahl, *Democracy and Its Critics* (New Haven, CT: Yale University Press, 1989), 2.

4 Dahl, *Democracy and Its Critics*, 2.

5 Dahl, *Democracy and Its Critics*, 108–9.

6 Dahl, *Democracy and Its Critics*, VII.

7 Dahl, *Democracy and Its Critics*, 328.

SECTION 1
INFLUENCES

MODULE 1
THE AUTHOR AND THE
HISTORICAL CONTEXT

KEY POINTS

- The American political scientist Robert A. Dahl believed modern democracy* to be based on the concept of polyarchy:* a word Dahl coined to designate "the rule of the many," as opposed to oligarchy* ("the rule of the few").

- Dahl's contact with "plain ordinary human beings" made him aware of the importance of information and education in enabling people to act in their self-interest.

- Dahl was writing in an era when democratic ideas were becoming increasingly accepted.

Why Read This Text?

Democracy and Its Critics offers an account of Robert A. Dahl's democratic thinking developed over the course of his academic career from the 1950s to the publication of the book in 1989.[1] It made an important contribution to democracy theory—that is, the development of ideas intended to explain how certain causes lead to certain effects. The book has become an introductory university text and a modern classic, still widely cited and discussed.

Dahl wanted *Democracy and Its Critics* to interpret and defend democratic theory and practice in a way that was relevant to the modern world.[2] This meant he had to respond to problems identified by critics of democracy, including the idea that the public is not capable of genuinely representing its own interests.

Decades earlier, Dahl began using the term "polyarchy" to describe a system where citizens pursue their goals in an organized way by

> **❝ I had this sense that ideas about democracy … from Aristotle and Plato onward … were inadequate. ❞**
> Robert A. Dahl, *A Conversation with Robert A. Dahl*

banding together in interest groups, such as trade unions, religious bodies, political parties, and the like.[3] He believed modern democracies function through a polyarchical clash of ideas, with different viewpoints supported by competing interest groups. In *Democracy and Its Critics*, Dahl tested the basic assumptions of democratic theory, then outlined the future directions he believes democracy should take, arguing that it would become more robust in existing democratic states and spread to nondemocratic states.

Author's Life

The American political scientist Robert Alan Dahl was born in Iowa in 1915, and grew up in a small town in Alaska. He earned a PhD in political science in 1940 at Yale University and then spent his entire academic career at the university, becoming Eugene Meyer Professor of Political Science in 1955. In 1964 he was named a Sterling Professor, the highest academic rank at Yale. From 1966 to 1967 he served as president of the American Political Science Association (APSA),* a professional organization for political science scholars. Dahl retired in 1989 but continued writing for another quarter century—his final book, *On Political Equality*, was published in 2006. Dahl died in 2014, at the age of 98.

Dahl has said that his interest in democracy was driven by his experience of growing up in a small town in Alaska. From the age of 12, his summers were spent working on the docks alongside longshore workers,* loading and unloading ships' cargo. Together with his military service and early experience of small town life, this gave him a deep respect for the common sense and abilities of what he called "plain ordinary human beings." Dahl also grew to appreciate the importance of information and education in helping people protect their own self-interests.

Democracy and Its Critics was published in 1989, not long after Dahl retired. The book explains his democratic thinking as it developed over the course of what was then a 50-year career as a political theorist. Dahl says that much of what he had written in the preceding decade dealt with the problems discussed in the book, and that the book reuses parts of his prior publications in revised form.[4]

Author's Background

Dahl spent much of his academic career trying to understand and explain the inner workings of democracy. He wanted to study the real extent of democratization in the world, and knew that to do so he first needed to define modern democracy and describe how it differs from the classical understanding of democracy.

Dahl's career coincided with the Cold War,* the period from about 1947 to 1991 when the world's two global superpowers, the United States and the Soviet Union,* offered competing visions of how the world should be governed. The United States favored democracy, while the Soviet Union favored communism,* a system where the government largely controls property and the economy. Dahl's early publications explored the role of democracy in the United States, particularly *Who Governs?* (1961), which used New Haven, Connecticut (where Yale University is located) as a case study. *Democracy and its Critics* was published in 1989, toward the end of both Dahl's career and the Cold War. Dahl recognized that "an unprecedented global expansion in the acceptability of democratic ideas"[5] was already happening, but he could not have known how rapidly the pace was going to quicken.

The geographic and political landscape of Europe was about to be profoundly transformed as the Eastern Bloc* countries (that is, the

Soviet-dominated states of Central and Eastern Europe) shed their communist governments. The transformation started abruptly in 1989 following the fall of the Berlin Wall,* a powerful symbol of Soviet power that separated the German city of Berlin into two parts, one communist, the other a democracy functioning on governmental principles common to other Western nations. In 1991 the Soviet Union's government collapsed, ending the Cold War and allowing many formerly communist countries to become democracies.

Samuel Huntington,* another American political scientist, later described this phenomenon as the "third wave" of democracy in his book *The Third Wave: Democratization in the Late Twentieth Century* (1991). For Huntington, the first wave of democracy followed the establishment of broad voting rights in the United States and other democracies in the early 1800s, with the second wave coming after the Allied victory in World War II. Huntington argued that starting in 1974, when Portugal became a democracy, the rate at which countries transitioned to democracy increased, with nearly 30 countries in Latin America, Asia, and the Middle East shedding authoritarian forms of government[6] (that is, forms of government under which citizens are subject to frequently oppressive state control). This rapid change, he argued, constituted the third wave.

NOTES

1   Robert A. Dahl, *Democracy and Its Critics* (New Haven, CT: Yale University Press, 1989).

2   Dahl, *Democracy and Its Critics*, 2.

3   See Robert A. Dahl, *A Preface to Democratic Theory* (Chicago: University of Chicago Press, 1956), 133.

4   Dahl, *Democracy and Its Critics*, vii.

5   Dahl, *Democracy and Its Critics*, 2.

6   Samuel Huntington, *The Third Wave: Democratization in the Late Twentieth Century* (Norman: University of Oklahoma Press, 1993), 280.

MODULE 2
ACADEMIC CONTEXT

KEY POINTS

- *Democracy and Its Critics* employs both comparative politics* (examining the difference between political systems) and political theory* (considering the nature of political systems).

- Robert A. Dahl's work draws on discussions about democracy* that go back more than 2,000 years, to the ancient Greeks.

- The revolutions in the late 1700s in America and France sparked another important wave of thinking about democracy.

The Work in its Context

Robert A. Dahl's *Democracy and Its Critics* is an exercise both in comparative politics (a method of political analysis) and political theory (a logical system of explanation). Some of its chapters, such as his exploration of the development of polyarchy* ("the rule of the many"), use elements of both disciplines.[1]

Comparative politics involves comparing political patterns in two or more countries. It looks at how constitutional designs, election systems, and other arrangements influence political and economic outcomes.[2] The method goes beyond mere description. It compares two very similar (or very different) cases, and identifies the variables between them—in this case, important differences and similarities. Dahl identified variables in 20 counties to see what conditions favored the development of polyarchy.[3]

❝ It will be obvious to the reader that my greatest debt, and most long-lasting one, is to the extraordinary thinkers from Socrates onwards who have engaged in the everlasting debates about democracy. ❞

Robert A. Dahl, *Democracy and Its Critics*

Dahl's text also has elements of political theory, which focuses "on the nature and structure of political practices, processes and institutions."[4] The book uses political theory to study how the political system works, and to explore how human beings can "live good and just lives within a political community."[5] *Democracy and Its Critics* considers what is meant by the "common good," and discusses the conditions that lead to polyarchy, and how polyarchy develops.[6]

Overview of the Field

Democracy and Its Critics is part of a 2,000-year-old debate about democracy, the study of which has endured as long as it has existed as a political system. One of the first studies of real-world democracy was the Greek philosopher Aristotle's* *Politics*, probably composed in the mid-300s B.C.E. Aristotle described three kinds of political organization:

- Rule by one (*kingship* when it was just; *tyranny* when it was not)
- Rule by few (*aristocracy** when it was just, *oligarchy** when it was not)
- Rule by the many (*polity** when it was just, *democracy* when it was not).

The word "polity" today is a general term for any system of government, but Aristotle used it to mean a balanced system combining oligarchy and democracy.

Aristotle thought democracy an improper form of political organization, believing it unjust that the whims of the many could govern the city. He described Athens at its most democratic as an "extreme democracy in which the [citizenry] considers itself above the laws."[7] Aristotle believed the best possible political system was a just kingship or aristocracy; in these cases, the great majority of the people would have their lives organized for them by their leaders, who presumably were wise and just. This "first best" organization, Aristotle admits, was unlikely to exist. His "second best" option was polity, a system that gives power both to the wealthy oligarchy and to the poorer citizens. Aristotle believed this would lead to a balance that was fairer than either oligarchy or democracy.

Commentary on democracy and democratic thought flourished during the Enlightenment* (the period in the seventeenth and eighteenth centuries when traditional authority was challenged by education, science and reason). The British American philosopher and revolutionary Thomas Paine* argued that only a democratic system could preserve freedom and respect the fundamental equality of all people. Key to this debate, according to Paine, was the separation between the state and society—"society is produced by our wants, and government by our wickedness."[8]

Paine believed the American* and French* Revolutions of the late 1700s ushered in an era where government would respect universal truths about the people it governs and its role with respect to those people.[9] He wanted a system where government exists only to ensure people do not violate one another's rights, and where the source of government's power is the "nation" (that is, all the people). In such a system, he believed democracy is the only way government can avoid unjustly giving some people (for example, a king) more rights than others.

However, other respected thinkers over the years have criticized democracy. In his *Civil Disobedience* (1849), the American philosopher

Henry David Thoreau* asked if democracy is democratic. Does it successfully protect the governed from their government? Thoreau suggested that "the many" possess no special wisdom just because of their numbers. "Even voting for the right is doing nothing for it," he wrote. "It is only expressing to men feebly your desire that it should prevail."[10] Thoreau believed democracy allowed people to be indifferent to genuinely important questions. Instead of acting on what they believe is right, people in a democracy merely say what they think and consider themselves done with the matter.

Academic Influences

In the acknowledgements of *Democracy and Its Critics*, Dahl states his intellectual debt to earlier thinkers about democracy, particularly the Greek philosopher Socrates.*[11] He was influenced by philosophers who focused on who should be allowed to vote in a democracy, like John Locke* of England and Jean-Jacques Rousseau* of France, and drew from the Greek philosopher Plato's* *Republic* (about 380 B.C.E.) when examining alternatives to a democratic form of government.[12]

Dahl's theory of democracy is based on two ideas:

- "Equal intrinsic worth,"* meaning each human is worth as much as every other human
- "Personal autonomy,"* meaning people set and pursue their own agendas based on their own wants and needs.

Locke declared that "no one can be … subjected to the Political Power of another without his own consent."[13] This idea is the fundamental basis for judging democracies. Dahl does not always agree with every element of classical theories of democracy—particularly unrealistic things like total citizen participation at all times.

Finally, we find clear influences of Alexis de Tocqueville,* a French political thinker who wrote *Democracy in America* in 1835 after a visit to the young United States. One of Tocqueville's interests was the many groups or associations formed among democratic citizens. "Americans of all ages, conditions, and all dispositions constantly unite together," he writes, for many reasons (religion, trade union, moral, and so on), and to many ends (political agitation, consciousness raising, networking, and the like), and are able to influence government together.[14] These associations do not weaken democracy, but rather provide a way for citizens to become more involved and effective members of the democracy. Dahl's concept of the polyarchy appears to build on this insight from Tocqueville.

NOTES

1   Robert A. Dahl, *Democracy and Its Critics* (New Haven, CT: Yale University Press, 1989), 232–43.

2   G. Helme and Steven Levitsky, "Informal Institutions and Comparative Politics, " *Perspectives on Politics* 2, no. 4 (2004): 725.

3   See Dahl, *Democracy and Its Critics*, 239.

4   David Held, *Political Theory and the Modern State* (New York: John Wiley & Sons, 2013), 3.

5   Richard J. Bernstein, *The Restructuring of Social and Political Theory* (Philadelphia: University of Pennsylvania Press, 1978), xxii.

6   See Dahl, *Democracy and Its Critics*, 239, 280–98.

7   Aristotle, *Politics* (London: Penguin Group, 1992), 1292a5–33.

8   Thomas Paine, "Common Sense," in *Rights of Man, Common Sense, and Other Political Writings* (Oxford: Oxford University Press, 2009), 5.

9   Paine, *Rights of Man*, 67.

10 Henry David Thoreau, *Civil Disobedience* (London: Dover Publications, 1993), 5.

11 Dahl, *Democracy and Its Critics*, vii.

12 See Dahl, *Democracy and Its Critics*, 52, 124.

13 John Locke, *Second Treatise of Government* (New York: Hackett Publishing, 1980), 348.

14 Alexis de Tocqueville, *Democracy in America* (London: Penguin Group,

MODULE 3
THE PROBLEM

KEY POINTS

- When Robert A. Dahl wrote *Democracy and Its Critics*, academics were researching whether the United States could be properly considered a pluralist* democracy* (that is, a democracy with multiple competing centers of power, supporting a marketplace of ideas).

- Some academics argued that gross inequalities in the United States meant it could no longer be considered a pluralist democracy.

- In *Democracy and Its Critics*, Dahl sought to design a society of political equals.

Core Question

Robert A. Dahl's *Democracy and Its Critics* addresses two core questions. The first is "What are the limits and possibilities of democracy?" Addressing it, Dahl considers the philosophical foundations and practical applications of democracy, and responds to those who criticize it as a system. The second question, which comes at the end of the book, is, "Is a 'third democratic transformation' within reach, and is some specific effort needed to achieve it?"[1]

In the decades before *Democracy and Its Critics* was published, some people raised doubts about whether the United States could properly be considered a pluralist democracy. They argued that America's economic and social system of capitalism* had given rise to gross inequalities of wealth, income, and power.[2] In *Democracy and Its Critics*, Dahl responds to these concerns as he seeks to design a society of political equals, arguing that legal and constitutional arrangements should be put in place to protect political equality.[3]

❝ Is a third [democratic] transformation now within reach? Even if it is, ought we make an effort to achieve it? ...To answer [these questions] we need to understand not only why democracy is desirable but what its limits and possibilities are. ❞

Robert A. Dahl, *Democracy and Its Critics*

The Participants

Theories about democracy tend to range from populist* to elitist.* The more populist thinkers assume the public is competent to rule itself, and that it should have authority to do so. The more elitist thinkers assume the public is not competent to rule itself, and that democracy is actually a process of elites bargaining with other elites, leaving only a minimal role for true popular rule.

Two American political scientists conducted one of the most important discussions on this subject in the twentieth century—the so-called "Lippmann-Dewey debate."* Walter Lippmann,* an elite theorist, and John Dewey,* a populist theorist, exchanged views through books and articles about the nature of democracy.

Lippmann argued in his book *Public Opinion* (1922) that citizens make decisions not on the basis of reality, but on the "pictures inside [their] heads"—an interpretation of reality that may not match actual reality.[4] Lippmann believed this is a major challenge for democracy because, in a "complicated civilization," voters will not be completely informed of a "world beyond their reach."[5] Ultimately, he believed we cannot depend on people to reach the common interest through voting since we vote on the basis of imaginary symbols.[6] It takes enormous expertise and full-time dedication to make "unseen facts intelligible," he wrote. To think the public or their representatives can acquire an "omnipotent opinion about public affairs" is "an intolerable and unworkable fiction."[7]

Dewey argued that the relationship between the public and the state was not as clearly divided as Lippmann suggests. He wrote that in debating about democracy, the most important "quality presented is not authorship but authority."[8] In other words, the public should not merely be seen as the best *author* of policy, but rather, as the *authority* that grants power and regulates how and why power is applied. "Dewey's point," argues the American scholar Melvin Rogers,* "is that the public is that space in which the democratic state attempts to see widely and feel deeply in order to make an informed judgment."[9]

The Contemporary Debate

Dahl saw himself entering a similar debate. His intention was to mount a defense of democracy against both the anarchist* school, a position founded on the abolition of state government altogether, represented by the American economist Richard Wolff,* and a school of thought similar to Lippmann's called "guardianship,"* represented by Joseph Schumpeter,* an Austrian American political scientist.

Wolff argued that a "morally legitimate state was a logical impossibility" because states tell people what to do. Wolff believed people cannot reasonably do what a state commands unless they believe they ought to do it—which means the state's command is unnecessary.[10] This is similar to earlier work by American philosopher Henry David Thoreau,* who rejected the authority of the state to legislate against the moral judgments of individuals. Dahl rejects this argument as unrealistic in the real world. For him, except in "extraordinary circumstances rarely attainable" given the size and complexity of modern societies, "if we wish to maximize our autonomy our only reasonable and responsible choice is to seek the best possible state."[11]

Joseph Schumpeter, on the other hand, advocated what Dahl called the "guardianship" view of democracy. "Democracy does not mean and cannot mean," Schumpeter argued, that "the people actually rule in any obvious sense," but rather, "only that the people have the opportunity of accepting or refusing the men who are to rule them."[12] Dahl calls these leaders "guardians," and believes that for this kind of system to be acceptable, there must be a "science of ruling ... composed of rationally unquestionable and objectively determined truths." This science would be comparable to the laws of physics, and require expertise to understand and use.[13]

For Dahl, "both moral understanding and instrumental knowledge are always necessary for policy judgments." But since neither is enough alone, a just system requires both moral decision-making and a general public agreement, reached after debate, on what the state *should* do.[14]

NOTES

1   Robert A. Dahl, *Democracy and Its Critics* (New Haven, CT: Yale University Press, 1989), 2.

2   John F. Manley, "Neo-Pluralism: A Class Analysis of Pluralism I and Pluralism II," *The American Political Science Review* 77, no. 2 (1983): 382.

3   Dahl, *Democracy and Its Critics*, 323, 326.

4   Walter Lippmann, *Public Opinion* (New York: Harcourt, Brace, 1922), 32.

5   Lippmann, *Public Opinion*, 32.

6   Lippmann, *Public Opinion*, 221.

7   Lippmann, *Public Opinion*, 18.

8   John Dewey, *The Public and its Problems: An Essay in Political Inquiry* (University Park: University of Pennsylvania Press, 2012), 26.

9   Melvin L. Rogers, introduction to Dewey, *The Public and Its Problems*, 27.

10 Robert Wolff, *In Defense of Anarchism* (London: University of California Press, 1998), VII.

11 Dahl, *Democracy and its Critics*, 49.

12 Joseph Schumpeter, *Capitalism, Socialism, and Democracy* (London: Routledge, 1976), 284–5.

13 Dahl, *Democracy and its Critics*, 66.

14 Dahl, *Democracy and its Critics*, 69.

MODULE 4
THE AUTHOR'S CONTRIBUTION

KEY POINTS

- Robert A. Dahl described democratic theory* and practice in a way relevant to modern democracies, and focused on problems that democratic theorists fail to address.

- *Democracy and Its Critics* brought together ideas that Dahl had written about for nearly four decades—notably the idea of polyarchy* ("rule by the many").

- Dahl believed most modern "democracies" were actually polyarchies, including the United States and United Kingdom.

Author's Aims

In *Democracy and Its Critics*, Robert A. Dahl aims to "set out an interpretation of democratic theory and practice, including the limits and possibilities of democracy* that is relevant to the kind of world in which we live or are likely to live in the foreseeable future."[1] Everybody recognizes the idea of democracy, but Dahl argues that in the modern world it is a vague term without a clearly defined meaning. To what extent, he asks, are democracies "democratic?"

The term "democracy" has been applied to a range of political systems, many of which have clearly nondemocratic tendencies. Dahl writes that democracy is now "not so much a term of restricted and specific meaning as a vague endorsement of a popular idea."[2] So he set out to describe the features of real, existing democracies in the world at that time. He labels these societies polyarchies, from the Greek words for "many" and "rule," and then discusses how polyarchies can move closer to democratic ideals. He gives the United Kingdom and the United

> ❝ What might loosely be called democratic theory ... depends on assumptions and premises that uncritical advocates have shied away from exploring, or in some cases even openly acknowledging. ❞
> Robert A. Dahl, *Democracy and Its Critics*

States as examples of polyarchies, saying they are both equally democratic, despite the fact that the UK has an unelected queen.

Approach

In *Democracy and Its Critics*, Dahl focuses on problems that advocates of democracy usually avoid or hide. These problems, he says, form "a vaguely perceived shadow theory that forever dogs the footsteps of explicit, public theories of democracy."[3] This "shadow" theory complicates the question of what "the people" means. "Democracy" means "rule by the people"—but what people, and whom do they rule? Dahl asks: "Why should Americans constitute 'a people' and their neighbors the Canadians and Mexicans separate peoples?"[4] Dahl aims to build a ground-up theory by exploring how the "shadow theory" avoided these fundamental questions.

He starts by identifying the most important influences on modern democracy:

- The philosophers of Ancient Greece, especially Socrates,* Plato* and Aristotle*
- A republican* tradition, in which people are governed by elected leaders under the rule of law, rather than by a monarch or tyrant
- The idea and institutions of representative government,* in which elected representatives exercise power
- The logic of political equality*—the possibility of someone from any section of society wielding political power.

This allows him to discuss each source of influence separately.[5]

Dahl then proceeds to explore two critiques of democracy: anarchism* and guardianship.* He examines problems in the democratic process, asking whether there is some alternative system that matches democracy's moral standards and values.[6] He then spells out the limits and possibilities of democracy[7] before sketching the future directions the system, in his view, should take.[8]

Contribution in Context

In *Democracy and Its Critics*, Dahl brought together and strengthened ideas about democracy he had been describing for nearly four decades. The book follows his long-standing research habit: to look at democracy in practice, rather than to discuss theoretical, ideal democracies.

Dahl and the American political scientist Charles E. Lindblom* first introduced the concept of polyarchy in their 1953 text *Politics, Economics and Welfare*.[9] It argued that all democracies share "polyarchical" tendencies (rule by many), but act out these tendencies in different ways. Later on, Dahl's *Who Governs?* (1961) offered a case study of polyarchy, examining the local democracy in New Haven, Connecticut, where Yale University is located. He built on this in his later important works on polyarchy. In *Polyarchy: Participation and Opposition* (1971), for example, he examined the conditions needed for a polyarchic system to be started.[10] *Democracy and Its Critics* builds on all these works, using the idea of polyarchy to distinguish between an ideal, theoretical democracy and a real, existing democracy.

Democracy and Its Critics therefore provides both a summing-up and a further development of Dahl's unique approach to his research.[11] Dahl's original thinking about democratic theory has made *Democracy and Its Critics* one of the most important books in the study of modern

democracy.
NOTES

1   Robert A. Dahl, *Democracy and Its Critics* (New Haven, CT: Yale University Press, 1989), 2.

2   Dahl, *Democracy and Its Critics*, 2.

3   Dahl, *Democracy and Its Critics*, 3.

4   Dahl, *Democracy and its Critics*, 3.

5   Dahl, *Democracy and Its Critics*, 13–33.

6   Dahl, *Democracy and Its Critics*, 135–209.

7   Dahl, *Democracy and Its Critics*, 213–308.

8   Dahl, *Democracy and Its Critics*, 311–41.

9   Robert A. Dahl and Charles E. Lindblom, *Politics, Economics, and Welfare* (New Brunswick, NJ, and London: Transaction Publishers, 1953).

10 Robert A. Dahl, *Polyarchy: Participation and Opposition* (New Haven, CT: Yale University Press, 1971).

11 See Robert A. Dahl and Margaret Levi, "A Conversation with Robert A. Dahl," *Annual Review of Political Science* 12 (2009): 1–9.

SECTION 2
IDEAS

MODULE 5
MAIN IDEAS

KEY POINTS

- Robert A. Dahl explores three themes in *Democracy and Its Critics*: a vast global expansion of the acceptability of democratic* ideas; the problems present in democratic ideas and practices; and the need to show that democracy* is the best form of government.

- Dahl's main argument was that real, existing democracies are polyarchies* that differ from classical democratic theory,* and that an interpretation of democratic theory and practice must account for that.

- Dahl presented his main argument by suggesting how polyarchies could develop into stronger democracies. He laid out ways to evaluate democracies and addresses objections to democracy.

Key Themes

The main argument in Robert A. Dahl's *Democracy and Its Critics* is that modern democracies are, in fact, polyarchies that differ from the traditional understanding of democracy. Dahl examines both whether democracy is the best possible political system, and the extent to which existing political structures meet the requirements of a best possible system. If it is worth making an effort to transform democracy, we must first understand why democracy is desirable, and how democratic ideas "come through" in polyarchies.[1]

To understand the difference between democracy and polyarchy, we need to start with the distinction between polyarchy— "government by minorities"—and oligarchy,* or dictatorship— "government by a minority."[2] "Government by minorities" means

> **❝** My aim in this book is to set out an interpretation of democratic theory and practice, including the limits and possibilities of democracy, that is relevant to the kind of world in which we live or are likely to live in the foreseeable future. **❞**
>
> Robert A. Dahl, *Democracy and Its Critics*

that different interest groups, such as trade unions, religious groups, or residents of a particular region, battle for influence over the government. Polyarchy is not "majority rule" but, rather, it is a system where multiple minority or interest groups jockey for position. The standards Dahl proposed for a country to qualify as a polyarchy are:

- Elected officials control policy-making
- Free and fair elections of officials
- Inclusive suffrage* (the right to vote)
- The right to run for office
- Freedom of speech
- Alternative information is available
- People can form political groups with autonomy*—the freedom to act independently.[3]

We understand that majorities rule in a democracy—but Dahl argued that this is true only in the limited sense that the majority of the people must provide "the underlying consensus on policy." This is because "disputes over policy alternatives are nearly always disputes over a set of alternatives that have always been winnowed down to those within a broad area of basic agreement."[4]

Exploring the Ideas

To justify democracy as a system, Dahl starts with the assumption that in order to live together, members of any association or group need a process to make decisions that are binding on the entire group. Dahl describes two foundations for democracy. The first is the principle of equal consideration of interests,* according to which "during a process of political decision-making, the interests of every person who is subject to the decision must ... be accurately interpreted and made known."[5] The second is the presumption of personal autonomy,* according to which each adult person should have the right to judge whether or not a policy is in his or her best interest.

Together, these premises led Dahl to adopt the strong principle of equality:* "every adult member of an association is sufficiently well qualified ... to participate in making binding collective decisions that affect his or her good or interests, that is, to be a full citizen of the demos*... [When] binding decisions are made, no citizen's claims as to the laws, rules and policies to be adopted are to be counted as superior to the claims of any other citizen."[6] ("Demos" is an ancient Greek term for the population of a city or state. Modern writers use it to mean "common people.")

Dahl lays down five standards as ideals against which democracies should be judged:

- *Effective participation*—citizens have adequate, equal opportunities for expressing their preferences for the final outcome throughout the decision-making process.
- *Voting equality*—at the decision-making stage, "each citizen must be ensured an equal opportunity to express a choice that will be counted as equal in weight to the choice expressed by any other citizen."[7]
- *Enlightened understanding**—"each citizen ought to have adequate and equal opportunities for discovering" the choices that are in the citizen's interest.[8]
- *Control of the agenda*—"the demos must have the exclusive opportunity to decide which matters will be decided by the democratic process."[9]

- *Inclusiveness of participation*—"the demos must include all adult members of the association," except transients and people who are mentally incapable of participating.[10]

According to Dahl, any political process that meets these standards would be a perfect democratic process, and its government would therefore be democratic.[11]

Language and Expression

Dahl's language in *Democracy and Its Critics* is fluid and easy to follow. This suggests that he intended the work to reach readers beyond academia, and to be easily accessible to policymakers and interested members of the general public. To help readers understand the complex debates between different schools of thought, Dahl uses the form of imagined dialogue between people with conflicting political ideologies. For instance, the text features a conversation between a democrat* and an anarchist* (someone who believes that people should organize themselves without any of the mechanisms that constitute government by the state)[12] and a discussion between the French philosopher Jean-Jacques Rousseau* and James Madison*— the primary author of the United States Constitution (the document setting out the aims, laws, and principles of the government), a man who later became president.[13]

Yet despite Dahl's intentions, *Democracy and Its Critics* has had more impact in academia than in the realm of public policy. There is no evidence that the text has influenced politicians or the military, but other scholars have used Dahl's definition of polyarchy as a basis for expanding on his work. The political scientists Michael Coppedge* of the United States and Wolfgang H. Reinicke* of Germany propose using Dahl's definition of polyarchy to measure whether different political systems meet the minimum requirements for democracy.[14] American co-authors Philippe Schmitter* and

Terry Lynn Karl* have worked to develop Dahl's definition further, using it as a jumping-off point for new ideas.[15]

NOTES

1   Robert A. Dahl, *Democracy and Its Critics* (New Haven, CT: Yale University Press, 1989), 2.

2   Robert A. Dahl, *A Preface to Democratic Theory* (Chicago: University of Chicago Press, 1956), 133.

3   Dahl, *Democracy and Its Critics*, 221.

4   Dahl, *A Preface,* 132–3.

5   Dahl, *Democracy and Its Critics*, 86.

6   Dahl, *Democracy and Its Critics*, 105.

7   Dahl, *Democracy and Its Critics*, 109.

8   Dahl, *Democracy and Its Critics*, 112.

9   Dahl, *Democracy and Its Critics*, 113.

10 Dahl, *Democracy and Its Critics*, 129.

11 Dahl, *Democracy and Its Critics*, 108–9.

12 See Dahl, *Democracy and Its Critics*, 39–40.

13 See Dahl, *Democracy and Its Critics*, 226–9.

14 Michael Coppedge and Wolfgang H. Reinicke, "Measuring Polyarchy," *Studies in Comparative International Development* 25, no. 1 (1990): 51–72.

15 Philippe C. Schmitter and Terry Lynn Karl, "What democracy is ... and is not," *Journal of Democracy* 2, no. 3 (1991): 75–88.

MODULE 6
SECONDARY IDEAS

KEY POINTS

- Robert A. Dahl argues that democracy* as a system must be defined and justified, and that economic enterprises should be democratized.

- Dahl's call to democratize economic enterprises is not central to his core argument.

- Dahl's arguments have found greater influence since the global economic recession* that began in 2007–8.

Other Ideas

One key idea in Robert A. Dahl's *Democracy and Its Critics* is that democracy has undergone two transformations, and may still undergo a third.

The first democratic transformation occurred in ancient Greece and Rome, where the notion of democracy was born: "What happened," Dahl explains, "was that several city-states [historically governed by] various undemocratic rulers … were transformed into a system in which a substantial number of free, adult males" claimed authority to govern themselves and their society.[1] This vision of democracy was also based on an ancient Greek ideal of political life—namely, political life being "an extension of, and harmonious with, oneself … happiness is united with virtue, virtue with justice, and justice with happiness."[2]

Next came the transfer of democracy from the city-state to the nation-state in the nineteenth century. "The second transformation simultaneously expanded and contracted the limits of democracy," argues Dahl. The direct democracy of ancient Greece, where all

> **❝** [Even] if we cannot justify democracy by demonstrating that it can be derived from 'objectively true' moral absolutes, we can, I believe, justify it on grounds that satisfactorily withstand tests of reason and experience. **❞**
>
> Robert A. Dahl, *Democracy and Its Critics*

citizens voted on all proposals, was replaced by representation,* where a broader group of citizens vote for people to speak on their behalf. This meant that while some citizens' participation in the political process decreased, more citizens were able to participate.[3]

Exploring the Ideas

Dahl believes that a possible third democratic transformation might yet occur. Democratic transitions would occur in nondemocratic countries, and changes in the "scale" of politics would expand in democratic states. In essence, Dahl is interested in examining the breadth (the international increase or decrease) and depth (the level of participation in a country) of democracy in the future.

Dahl argues that democratic transitions in nondemocratic countries could move in either direction. Democracy could expand "as the political institutions of more and more and more nondemocratic countries are transformed into polyarchy,"* or contract "as the conditions for polyarchy become more unfavorable" because leaders take stronger control.[4] Dahl discards the "temptation … to divide the world neatly into democracies, which are by assumption good, and nondemocracies, which are by assumption bad." He suggests instead that states should be evaluated based on the extent to which they are genuinely polyarchical. For example, a revolutionary nondemocratic regime might be a positive force in bringing about conditions for the development of polyarchy in future.[5] As unexpected as that may seem, Dahl reminded his readers that democratization is a slow process that may not yet be complete. In most Western nation states, it took centuries to develop.

Dahl's second point about the future of democracy involves the changing scale of politics. He hints about democracy expanding *beyond* the nation-state, arguing that the rise of international activities "reduces the capacity of the citizens of a country to exercise control over matters vitally important to them by means of their national government."[6] Dahl dismisses the possibility of a transnational world-democracy as unrealistic. He suggests instead that "in order to maintain the vitality of the democratic process" in the face of increasingly important transnational activities, "democratic institutions within countries would need to be improved." This would include deciding precisely how much authority states delegate to non-state actors.[7] This can be thought of as representation on another level—citizens elect representatives, who act as intermediaries between citizens and transnational organizations, which then act.

Overlooked

As a leading text on democracy, *Democracy and Its Critics* has been cited more than 7,300 times in scholarly literature, according to Google Scholar.[8] This means thousands of scholars have pored over his text and used it as a model for their own research. But despite such a high level of scrutiny, there is one area of *Democracy and Its Critics* that has been neglected by other scholars. There has been little scholarly discussion of Dahl's call for democratization to be extended to businesses in what he refers to as MDP societies*—societies that are modern, dynamic and pluralist* (modern, capable of change and having more than one center of power).[9]

Dahl said MDP societies have a relatively high level of income and wealth per capita (that is, per head of population), a high level of urbanization, great occupational diversity, extensive literacy, a small agricultural population, and an economic order where production is mainly carried out by self-directed firms oriented toward national and international markets. In these societies, Dahl argues, economic enterprises should change the way they work to become more polyarchical. He imagines a company where all the employees, in free and fair elections (that is, universal suffrage),* elected the company leadership, in which any employee could run for office, where employees had freedom of speech, freedom to form unions or other employee groups, and access to company records. Instead of being accountable to a board of directors and shareholders, the company would be accountable to its employees; this is the vision Dahl's offers.

The global economic recession that began in 2007–8 may have created an opportunity for research into Dahl's vision of democratizing businesses. For example, in September 2011, a group of people began a sit-in protest on Wall Street, the financial center of the United States. Their primary demands were democratization of the workplace and redistribution of economic wealth.[10] They became known as the Occupy movement,* and similar protests soon sprang up around the world.

NOTES

1   Robert A. Dahl, *Democracy and Its Critics* (New Haven, CT: Yale University Press, 1989), 13.

2   Dahl, *Democracy and its Critics*, 18.

3   Dahl, *Democracy and its Critics*, 318.

4   Dahl, *Democracy and its Critics*, 313–14.

5   Dahl, *Democracy and its Critics*, 316.

6   Dahl, *Democracy and its Critics*, 319.

7   Dahl, *Democracy and its Critics*, 320.

8   Google Scholar, https://scholar.google.com/
    scholar?q=%22democracy+and+its+critics%22+dahl&btnG=&hl=en&as_
    sdt=0%2C9, accessed September 18, 2015.

9   Dahl, *Democracy and Its Critics*, 327.

10 "About," Occupy Wall Street Movement, accessed September 9, 2015,
    http://occupywallst.org/about/.

MODULE 7
ACHIEVEMENT

KEY POINTS

- In order to make *Democracy and Its Critics* relevant to all governments, Robert A. Dahl established standards that could be used to consider political systems around the world.

- Dahl describes and explains all the major sources of thinking on democracy,* from the ancient Greeks to the twentieth century.

- Critics from a legal background have disputed some of Dahl's ideas, calling the book too vague and too simple.

Considering the Argument

Robert A. Dahl's aim in *Democracy and Its Critics* is to "set out an interpretation of democratic theory* and practice, including the limits and possibilities of democracy, that is relevant to the kind of world in which we live or are likely to live in the foreseeable future."[1] Dahl focuses on problems that promoters of democracy typically neglect or conceal, saying these problems form "a vaguely perceived shadow theory that forever dogs the footsteps of explicit, public theories of democracy."[2] By closely examining the details of this "shadow theory," Dahl sought to identify and explore the thinking and conditions on which a theory of democracy should be built.[3]

Dahl uses these goals to create a clear plan for *Democracy and Its Critics*. As we have seen, he starts by identifying the most important sources of modern democracy:

- The writings of philosophers of ancient Greece, especially Socrates,* Plato* and Aristotle*

> **❝** Time spent with *Democracy and Its Critics* will repay both the scholar and the general reader with insight into the issues of democratic theory that bear on the continual debate over the proper role of an independent judiciary in a democratic society **❞**
>
> Cary Coglianese, "Review of *Democracy and Its Critics* by Robert A. Dahl"

- A republican* tradition, in which people are governed by the rule of law, rather than by a monarch or tyrant
- The idea and institutions of representative government,* in which elected representatives exercise power
- The logic of political equality*—the possibility that someone from any section of society might wield political power.

This allowed him to explore each source individually.[4] Dahl described the conditions that justify a democratic political system, and outlined the limits and possibilities of democracy.[5] He then discussed the future directions that democracy, in his view, should take.[6]

In doing all this, Dahl achieved his goal of describing democratic theory and practice in a way that relates to real, existing political systems in the contemporary world. He also paid attention to criticisms of democracy that democracy theory had otherwise largely neglected.

Achievement in Context

Democracy and Its Critics incorporated Dahl's lifetime's work, then nearly four decades of writing on democratic theory. Many parts of Dahl's past publications were included, in a revised form, in the book. Dahl was studying and writing about some of his own theories.

Shortly after *Democracy and Its Critics* was published in 1989, interest in democratic theory increased rapidly after the fall of the Berlin Wall*—a conspicuous symbol of Soviet* influence in European politics—and the collapse of the communist* Soviet Union.

One aspect that aroused particular interest was Dahl's suggestion of the "minipopulus"* as a deliberative* body—people who would discuss important issues and try to persuade each other. Inspired by Dahl, scholars proposed several ways to form groups of citizens who could deliberate together. For example, theorists John S. Dryzek* and Robert E. Goodin* discussed in a series of articles their idea of "mini-publics," similar to Dahl's minipopuli but without authority to set its own agenda.[7] The function of a "mini-public" according to Dryzek and Goodin is more like a policy-improvement body, while Dahl's minipopulous would play a role in making policy decisions.

Limitations

Robert A. Dahl's *Democracy and Its Critics* is still significant today. He wanted the text to offer a universal democratic theory, so he established standards to evaluate any country's political system. His ideas are relevant around the world.

Democracy and Its Critics has been influential in the academic discipline of law. For example, the law scholar and political scientist Cary Coglianese* has related Dahl's work to the role of independent, unelected judges in a democracy: "Time spent with *Democracy and Its Critics* will repay both the scholar and the general reader with insight into the issues of democratic theory that bear on the continual debate over the proper role of an independent judiciary in a democratic society."[8]

Legal academics have also engaged with the text by criticizing Dahl's ideas about who is included in the demos*—the collection of common people whose opinions must be considered. Dahl believed "every adult subject to a government and its laws must be presumed to be qualified as … a member of the demos," except transients and persons with severe mental disabilities.[9] However, the American political scientist Elizabeth Cohen* believes the idea is too vague to guide legal practice. For example, the boundaries between childhood and adulthood are not clearly established; the definition of a transient is not clear; and most liberal democracies do not deprive the mentally impaired of citizenship rights.[10]

NOTES

1   Robert A. Dahl, *Democracy and Its Critics* (New Haven, CT: Yale University Press, 1989), 2.

2   Dahl, *Democracy and Its Critics*, 3.

3   Dahl, *Democracy and Its Critics*, 5.

4   Dahl, *Democracy and Its Critics*, 13–33.

5   Dahl, *Democracy and Its Critics*, 213–308.

6   Dahl, *Democracy and Its Critics*, 311–41.

7   Robert E. Goodin and John S. Dryzek, "Deliberative Impacts: The Macro-Political Uptake of Mini-Publics," *Politics and Society* 34, no. 2 (2006): 219–44; Robert E. Goodin and John S. Dryzek, "Making Use of Mini-publics," in *Innovating Democracy: Democratic Theory and Practice after the Deliberative Turn*, ed. Robert E. Goodin (Oxford: Oxford University Press, 2008), 11–37.

8   Cary Coglianese, "Review of *Democracy and Its Critics* by Robert A. Dahl," *Michigan Law Review* 88, no. 6 (1990): 1662–7.

9   Dahl, *Democracy and Its Critics*, 127–9.

10   Elizabeth F. Cohen, *Semi-Citizenship in Democratic Politics* (Cambridge: Cambridge University Press, 2009), 39.

MODULE 8
PLACE IN THE AUTHOR'S WORK

KEY POINTS

- Robert A. Dahl has been influential in political science since the 1950s, and has written on behavioralism* (in political science, the study of political behavior such as voting, public opinion, legislative behaviors, and nongovernmental associations and interest groups), power, and democracy.*

- *Democracy and Its Critics* examined real, existing democracies as opposed to idealized, theoretical democracies.

- While *Democracy and Its Critics* is a modern classic, Dahl had established his reputation as a leading political theorist before its publication.

Positioning

Robert A. Dahl's *Democracy and Its Critics* was published in 1989, not long after Dahl retired as a highly respected professor at Yale University. In the introduction, Dahl writes that much of what he had written in the previous decade dealt with the central issues in this book and that some parts of the text had been published in different form elsewhere.[1] The book is a product of a lifetime of work.

Dahl had been influential in the field of political science since the early 1950s, when he established himself as a leading scholar of the behavioralist school of thought.[2] This emphasized the importance of measurable actions in the study of political science.

Democracy and Its Critics uses Dahl's long-standing research practice, which was to examine real, existing democracies rather than idealized, theoretical democracies. Dahl refers to these real democracies as

> ❝ "[It's] all one big, long book. I'm always astonished when people see these great discontinuities. I think it's quite the other way around. ❞
>
> Robert A. Dahl, quoted in Nelson W. Polsby's, "Interview with Robert A. Dahl"

polyarchies,* a concept first introduced *Politics, Economics and Welfare* (1953), which Dahl co-wrote with the political scientist Charles E. Lindblom.* The idea informed Dahl's later works *A Preface to Democratic Theory* (1956) and *Who Governs?* (1961).

Integration

Having already established a reputation as a key democratic theorist of the pluralist* school of thought, Dahl used *Democracy and Its Critics* to bring together his entire body of work that stemmed from a career of studying democratic theory.* In *Who Governs?*,[3] for example, Dahl argued that the American democratic system is a pluralist system—meaning that there was no single power center and that power was shared among different interest groups. During the 1960s and 1970s, pluralist democracy came under heavy criticism from scholars who argued that there were important differences between the pluralist democratic model and the way that Western democracies actually worked.

In his later work, Dahl moved forward from his earlier democratic theory, which had largely defended and justified the existing system. Throughout his career he examined real, existing democracies, declaring them in fact to be polyarchies that fell short of genuine democratic ideals. In *Democracy and Its Critics*, Dahl develops this research practice further. He proposed certain standards for a country to be called a polyarchy, and a separate set of standards for a political process to be considered democratic. He then proposed ways that countries might close the gap between polyarchy and real democracy.

Dahl's body of work is intellectually clear and unified. He described his writing over his entire career as the equivalent of one long book, telling an interviewer in 1991: "In fact, I'm a little worried sometimes about that: that it's all one big, long book. I'm always astonished when people see these great discontinuities. I think it's quite the other way around."[4] However, Dahl also modified and updated some of his earlier conclusions from the 1960s, which had largely defended the existing political system. He gradually developed a more negative view of the American political system, for example.

Significance

Prior to the publication of *Democracy and Its Critics*, Dahl had already established himself as a leading political scientist and democracy theorist. He was particularly influential in describing the nature of political power. In 1957, Dahl said: "A has power over B to the extent that he can get B to do something that B would otherwise not do."[5] Using this definition, Dahl showed it was possible to compare the relative power of two or more people. As a real-world demonstration, he used the definition to rank members of the US Senate according to the power they had over laws dealing with foreign policy and taxes.[6]

Although *Democracy and Its Critics* is Dahl's most famous book, it would be misleading to describe it as his "best work." Dahl was perhaps the most influential democratic theorist in the world, and began having a huge impact on political science in the early 1950s. In this sense, *Democracy and Its Critics* brought together Dahl's well-known democratic theory as developed over the preceding decades.

NOTES

1   Robert A. Dahl, *Democracy and Its Critics* (New Haven, CT: Yale University Press, 1989), VII.

2   Robert A. Dahl, *Who Governs? Democracy and Power in an American City* (New Haven, CT: Yale University Press, 1961); *A Preface to Democratic Theory* (Chicago: University of Chicago Press, 2006); *Pluralist Democracy in the United States: Conflict and Consent* (Chicago: Rand McNally, 1967).

3   Robert A. Dahl, *Who Governs?*

4   Nelson W. Polsby, "Interview with Robert A. Dahl," in *Political Science in America: Oral Histories of a Discipline*, ed. Michael A. Baer et al. (Lexington: University Press of Kentucky, 1991), 175.

5   Robert A. Dahl, "The Concept of Power," *Behavioral Science* 2 (1957): 202–3.

6   Dahl, "The Concept of Power," 201.

SECTION 3
IMPACT

MODULE 9
THE FIRST RESPONSES

KEY POINTS

- In *Democracy and its Critics*, Dahl discusses two different forms of democracy:* aggregative* (emphasizing the counting of preferences, expressed through voting) and deliberative* (according to which voting alone is not enough—informed debate is necessary).

- Robert A. Dahl was criticized for supposedly putting forward an aggregative view of democracy; he disagreed, saying his view of democracy incorporated deliberation.

- Dahl responded to these and other critics in an academic journal as part of the lively debate that made *Democracy and Its Critics* a highly influential book.

Criticism

Robert A. Dahl's *Democracy and Its Critics* received an overwhelmingly favorable response. The *American Political Science Review* claimed that "Dahl has produced a work destined to become another classic."[1] Another reviewer noted the appeal of the book to lay audiences, noting that text "is written in a style that makes it accessible … to the intelligent general reader."[2] However, this does not mean that the book was without its critics.

Some of the criticism focused on differences between two schools of thought about what makes a democracy legitimate:

- "Aggregative democracy" is an understanding of democracy that emphasizes the collection and counting (aggregation) of preferences, expressed through voting.

- "Deliberative democracy" holds that voting alone is not enough. In this view, informed debate (or deliberation) is an important part of what makes a political process genuinely

> **❝ I think that a principal obstacle lies in Dahl's** *aggregative* **conception of democracy. ❞**
> Joshua Cohen, "Institutional Argument … Is Diminished by the Limited Examination of the Issues of Principle"

democratic.

The political theorist Joshua Cohen,* for example, questioned Dahl's attempts to show that democracy can exist along with other political values, like liberty, equality and the common good. He believed Dahl had put forward an aggregative view of democracy, focused merely on counting votes for predetermined issues. Cohen suggested a more deliberative model, believing that the values of liberty, equality and the common good required genuine popular participation in debating and framing the issues.[3]

Others criticized Dahl's notion of a democratic transformation. For Dahl, democracy had progressed and improved from ancient Greece to the Italian city-states in the ninth through fifteenth centuries, and finally to the nation-state and today's societies. The American political philosopher Jean Bethke Elshtain* said, "if things are, on the whole, so good, [why is there a] widespread perception of decay and decline?"[4] Elshtain thought democracy might be weakening; she found American cities, for example, to be increasingly powerless, as authority had shifted to state and national governments. For her, Dahl ignored the troubles of the American welfare state* (that is, the collection of laws and government programs designed to support people's well-being); finally, Elshtain said the development of the nation-states involved a great deal of violence, and accused Dahl of underestimating how this continues to affect the democratic project.

In a third line of criticism, the political scientist Jack Nagel* said there were gaps in *Democracy and Its Critics.*[5] Dahl was criticized for not addressing the unreasonable and non-rational factors that can affect political systems. He said Dahl failed to address whether democracy has an answer to the manipulation of feelings for political gain—for example, when election campaigns use misleading emotional symbols to try to change how people vote.[6]

Responses

In *The Journal of Politics*, Dahl responded to the criticisms of Cohen, Elshtain, and Nagel.[7]

He stated that he found Cohen's deliberative model of democracy highly attractive, and that his own model was not aggregative in the way he understood Cohen to use the term. Dahl agreed with Cohen that mere aggregation of votes was not enough for democratic decision-making, and that deliberation was also needed. Dahl also said that deliberation would be enhanced by his proposed "minipopulus"*—a deliberative body of about a thousand randomly selected citizens. A minipopulus would be formed to consider (that is, to deliberate on) a major issue for about a year before reaching a decision. Different minipopuli could be created to consider different issues. These would not replace legislative bodies, but would help inform legislative actions.[8]

Dahl agreed that *Democracy and Its Critics* had not addressed the questions raised by Elshtain. He said he had not intended the book to be specifically about American democracy and its particular problems. Instead, he wanted to offer a universal theory* based on the widest possible range of democratic ideas and experiences, both from today and from the past.[9]

Finally, Dahl agreed with Nagel that the book did not deal with every important aspect of democratic theory. He wrote: "Nagel's comments reassure me that the thrust of my argument will be clear to the attentive reader," though he acknowledges that disagreements are bound to happen.[10]

Conflict and Consensus

Despite Dahl's response, Cohen was not convinced. Cohen was a leading authority on deliberative democracy in the last decade of the twentieth century, when the idea of deliberative democracy was becoming more influential. The "deliberative turn" criticized "minimalist democracy," where "all it asks of its citizens is to cast a ballot from time to time." The minimalist model has no interest in the extent to which voters are informed by public debate with one another.[11]

The political scientists Amy Gutmann* and Dennis Thompson* suggested that the deliberative turn occurred largely because of changing beliefs about how democratically elected governments should work. They use the lead-up to the Iraq War* as an example, when President George W. Bush* and his advisors "recognized the need to justify the decision not only to the American people but also to the world community." Critics also made their views known, "challenging the administration on all its arguments in favor of going to war," in the belief that nonmilitary action might have controlled the threat.[12] Gutmann and Thompson say this is important because "both the advocates and the foes of the war acted as if they recognized an obligation to justify their views."[13] The increased legitimacy of deliberative democracy may explain why Dahl's response was to agree, and to argue that he was always a deliberative theorist.

NOTES

1   Lucian W. Pye, "Book Reviews: Political Theory," *American Political Science Review* 84, no. 2 (1990): 627.

2   J. Roland Pennock, "Review," *Political Theory* 18, no. 3 (1990): 512.

3   Joshua Cohen, "Institutional Argument ... Is Diminished by the Limited Examination of the Issues of Principle," *The Journal of Politics* 53, no. 1 (1991): 225.

4   Jean Bethke Elshtain, "If Things Are, on the Whole, so Good, Whence the

Widespread Perception of Decay and Decline?" *The Journal of Politics* 53, no. 1 (1991): 219.

5   Jack H. Nagel, "A Democrat First and Foremost, Rather than a Liberal in the Strict Sense," *The Journal of Politics* 53, no. 1 (1991): 215–18.

6   Nagel, "A Democrat," 217.

7   Robert A. Dahl, "A Rejoinder," *The Journal of Politics* 53, no. 1 (1991): 226–31.

8   Robert A. Dahl, *Democracy and Its Critics* (New Haven, CT: Yale University Press, 1989), 340.

9   Dahl, "A Rejoinder," 227.

10 Dahl, "A Rejoinder," 226.

11 Robert E. Goodin, *Innovating Democracy: Democratic Theory and Practice after the Deliberative Turn* (Oxford: Oxford University Press, 2008), 1.

12 Amy Gutmann and Dennis Thompson, *Why Deliberative Democracy?* (Princeton: Princeton University Press, 2004), 2.

13 Gutmann and Thompson, *Why Deliberative Democracy?*, 3.

MODULE 10
THE EVOLVING DEBATE

KEY POINTS

- *Democracy and Its Critics* established a model of an advanced democratic society.

- Robert A. Dahl's outline of a future democratic society has influenced the study of deliberative democracy*—a system in which informed debate is important to the process of reaching decisions.

- Dahl's idea of the minipopulus* has led to deliberative democrats proposing similar designs that rely on small groups of citizens, representative of the citizenry as a whole, deliberating on important issues.

Uses and Problems

Democracy and Its Critics built on Robert A. Dahl's existing democratic theory* to describe what an advanced democratic society would look like. Such a society would focus on narrowing the gap between policy elites*—the class of people permitted to decide policy—and the people as a whole. Dahl suggests that an advanced democratic country would actively try to reduce inequalities among citizens. Equal participation in political life can be affected by the distribution of economic resources, positions, opportunity, knowledge and information.[1] He also suggests creating deliberative bodies that would include a thousand randomly selected citizens—bodies he called minipopuli; each minipopulus would thoroughly debate a specific policy issue, helping to inform the decisions of the governmental bodies that debate and pass laws.

❝ The decisions of bodies with formal legal authority might be more widely respected across the rest of the macro-political system the more conspicuously they involve the deliberative engagement of a wide, representative group of ordinary citizens. ❞

Robert E. Goodwin and John S. Dryzek, "Making use of Mini-publics"

Dahl's outline of a future democratic society has greatly influenced the study of democratic theory. Deliberative democracy theorists have taken up Dahl's idea of the minipopulus and explored it in their own work. Scholars offered competing ways to create bodies of citizens who could deliberate together, and who were representative of the citizenry as whole. For example, John S. Dryzek* and Robert E. Goodin* have discussed what they call "mini-publics"—bodies of citizens who discuss policy issues and form opinions.[2]

Schools of Thought

In *Democracy and Its Critics*, Dahl takes a proceduralist* view of democracy*—he justifies democracy not through moral arguments, but by the favorable outcomes of democratic procedures.* These outcomes include:

- The provision of essential rights
- The avoidance of tyranny
- The promotion of freedom and moral autonomy
- The promotion of political equality—for Dahl, the most important outcome.

Later scholars have focused on the seven principles that Dahl describes for his ideal type of existing democracy (polyarchy):*

- Elected officials control policy-making
- Free and fair elections of officials

- Inclusive suffrage*
- The right to run for office
- Freedom of speech
- The availability of alternative information
- The ability to form autonomous (independent) political groups.[3]

The political scientists Michael Coppedge* and Wolfgang H. Reinicke* have developed a scale based on Dahl's notion of polyarchy to see how closely different political systems meet the minimum requirements for democracy.[4] (Although they took Dahl's definition of polyarchy from his book *Polyarchy: Participation and Opposition* (1971) as their starting-point, that definition is nearly identical to the one Dahl offered in *Democracy and Its Critics*.)[5]

Other scholarship has sought to enrich Dahl's definition, using it as a jumping-off point for new models. The political scientists Philippe Schmitter* and Terry Lynn Karl* made two additions to Dahl's list. They said "popularly elected officials must be able to exercise their constitutional powers without being subjected to overriding informal opposition from unelected officials," and that "the polity* must be self-governing, and able to act independently of constraints imposed by another overarching political system."[6] While this model retained Dahl's proceduralist concept of democracy, Schmitter and Karl rejected Dahl's introduction of the term "polyarchy." They wrote about "democracy," which they considered the "catchword of contemporary political discourse," believing that people identify with it.

In Current Scholarship

One part of Dahl's *Democracy and Its Critics* that has attracted particular attention is his solution for promoting democratic deliberation. In Dahl's sketch of an advanced democratic country, members of the minipopulus would deliberate policy issues with each other, using telecommunications. Each minipopulus would be in charge of one major issue that was important at that time to the demos*—the common people with a right to be heard.[7]

Dahl's idea of the minipopulus has inspired later designs by deliberative democrats. A range of proposals rely on small groups of citizens, representative of the people as a whole, deliberating together. Dryzek and Goodin discussed what they call "mini-publics," deliberative citizen forums that discuss policy issues and form opinions. They believe mini-publics can have real political impact, through measures like deliberative polls, consensus conferences, and citizens' juries.[8]

The communications scholar James S. Fishkin* has also designed a model of a "mini-public." In *Democracy and Deliberation*, Fishkin suggests a national caucus—bloc of voters—that includes a sample of American citizens. The caucus would be able to interact with presidential candidates at the beginning of the presidential primary* season (the period when candidates are selected to stand for election), and debate policy issues with the candidates and with each other. The delegates would then be polled on their preferences, to show what the electorate as a whole might think if given the opportunity for deliberation. As early as 1988, a year before the publication of *Democracy and Its Critics*, Fishkin's Center for Deliberative Polling at Stanford University set up so-called "deliberative polls." These bring together between 250 and 500 randomly selected citizens who hear evidence from—and pose questions to—experts on policy issues. The findings, published in Fishkin and Bruce Ackerman's* *Deliberation Day* (2004), suggested that this model be expanded across the US before national elections, inviting all citizens to participate.[9]

However, the mini-publics discussed by Dryzek and Goodin, as well as the deliberative polls of Fishkin and Ackerman, differ from Dahl's idea of the minipopulus. A basic idea of the minipopulus was that it would be able to raise issues for discussion, while mini-publics and deliberative polls would generally discuss predetermined policy issues.

NOTES

1   Robert A. Dahl, *Democracy and Its Critics* (New Haven, CT: Yale University Press, 1989), 324.

2   Robert E. Goodin and John S. Dryzek, "Deliberative Impacts: The Macro-Political Uptake of Mini-Publics," *Politics and Society* 34, no. 2 (2006): 219–44; Robert E. Goodin and John S. Dryzek, "Making Use of Mini-publics," in *Innovating Democracy: Democratic Theory and Practice after the Deliberative Turn*, ed. Robert E. Goodin (Oxford: Oxford University Press, 2008), 11–37.

3   Dahl, *Democracy and Its Critics*, 221.

4   Michael Coppedge and Wolfgang H. Reinicke, "Measuring Polyarchy," *Studies in Comparative International Development* 25, no. 1 (1990): 51–72.

5   Dahl, *Democracy and Its Critics*, 221.

6   Philippe C. Schmitter and Terry Lynn Karl, "What democracy is … and is not," *Journal of Democracy* 2, no. 3 (1991): 75–88.

7   Dahl, *Democracy and Its Critics*, 340.

8   Goodin and Dryzek, "Deliberative Impacts," 219–44; "Making Use of Mini-publics," 11–37.

9   Bruce A. Ackerman and James S. Fishkin, *Deliberation Day* (Yale University Press, 2004).

MODULE 11
IMPACT AND INFLUENCE TODAY

KEY POINTS

- *Democracy and Its Critics* is still relevant both for its democratic theory,* and its suggestions about how to make existing governments more democratic.

- *Democracy and Its Critics* has been interpreted by the American political theorist Joshua Cohen* as advocating aggregative democracy.*

- Cohen has responded to Dahl by outlining the five features that he thinks are important for deliberative democracy.*

Position

Robert A. Dahl's *Democracy and Its Critics* interprets democratic theory in a way that is relevant both today and in the future. His specific proposals to make nation-states in the world today more fully democratic have been influential. For instance, Dahl's suggestion that the minipopulus* be introduced into the democratic process continues to be debated among democratic theorists.

Dahl strongly believed that telecommunications technology could be used to increase democratization. He suggested his minipopuli could use digital technology in order to meet—and this was in 1989, before most people had heard of the Internet. The relationship between technological improvement and democratization is hotly debated today, showing Dahl's foresight when the book was published. For instance, the law scholar Cary Coglianese* has argued that information technology is unlikely to make policy-making more democratic; for him, although technology offers citizens increased access to rule-making information, it does not make that information easier to use.[1]

> **❝** We are pushed into [a] dilemma by a particular understanding of democracy, which I will call 'aggregative'—as distinct from deliberative. **❞**
> Joshua Cohen, "Procedure and Substance in Deliberative Democracy"

Interaction

American political theorist Joshua Cohen maintained his original criticism that Dahl's view of democracy* was aggregative—that it was based primarily on voting rather than on deliberation. He said Dahl's aggregative view focused on equal consideration for each member's interests* as the primary basis for declaring that a political process is democratic. This, he said, ignored other important elements of democracy.[2]

In his essay "Democracy and Liberty," Cohen continued to challenge the legitimacy of a purely procedural* understanding of democracy. In *Democracy and Its Critics*, Dahl justifies democracy not through moral arguments, but by the favorable outcomes of democratic procedures.* Cohen made the case for his deliberative view, arguing that a fair process is not enough. The deliberative view maintains that certain political values are essential elements of democracy, including political equality, religious and moral liberties, and the common good.[3]

Cohen proposed his own model of five main features of a deliberative democracy:

- A deliberative democracy is an ongoing and independent association, whose members expect it to continue into the indefinite future
- Free deliberation among equals is the basis of legitimacy
- A deliberative democracy is pluralistic* (constituted by multiple competing centers of power)

- The institutions in which deliberation occurs were created through a process of deliberation
- The members recognize one another as having deliberative ability.[4]

The Continuing Debate

Dahl's later work, especially his more philosophical *On Political Equality* (2006), suggested that Cohen's deliberative democracy is not as different from Dahl's own conception of democracy as it may seem. "It is an easily observable fact," Dahl argued, "that while a small minority of persons in democratic countries spend a large portion of their time seeking and employing political influence, the great majority of citizens" simply lack the time and resources. Dahl said this difference hurts the prospects for political equality,[5] especially when it is combined with a market economy.

Moreover, Dahl argued that political inequality among the citizens of a democratic country was produced through the "great inequalities in resources among citizens," which was an inevitable function of market capitalism.* People with fewer resources have less influence over the political process, and this damages the ideals of free deliberation and mutual recognition.[6] So Dahl's "ideal" democracy was not far off from Cohen's. But Dahl also believed that the size and complexity of political bodies, and the inequality caused by a market economy, limit the ability of some citizens to participate fully in the deliberative process.

NOTES

1   Cary Coglianese, "Weak Democracy, Strong Information: The Role of Information Technology in the Rulemaking Process," Public Law Working Paper, No. 07-04 (2007): 23.

2   Joshua Cohen, "Democracy and Liberty," in *Deliberative Democracy*, ed. Jon Elster (New York: Cambridge University Press, 1998), 187.

3   Cohen, "Democracy and Liberty," 187.

4   Joshua Cohen, "Deliberation and Democratic Legitimacy," in *Deliberative Democracy: Essays on Reason and Politics*, ed. James Bohman and William Rehg (Cambridge, MA: The MIT Press, 1997), 72–3.

5   Robert A. Dahl, *On Political Equality* (New Haven: Yale University Press, 2006), 56.

6   Dahl, *On Political Equality*, 67.

MODULE 12
WHERE NEXT?

KEY POINTS

- *Democracy and Its Critics* will remain relevant in debates about how existing governments can become more democratic.

- Robert A. Dahl's calls to democratize businesses may become increasingly relevant after the global economic recession* that began in 2007–8.

- *Democracy and Its Critics* is important for testing the foundations of democratic theory,* and for its arguments concerning the future of democracy.*

Potential

Robert A. Dahl's *Democracy and Its Critics*, published in 1989, continues to be a highly-respected work of democratic theory. It is likely to remain important in debates about democracy for years to come.

Dahl's idea of workplace democracy could be further developed by future scholarship. Dahl argues that the same democratic processes that govern nation-states should be used to manage economic enterprises (businesses or corporations).[1] The recent global economic recession has led to increased debate on this issue. Dahl suggests several specific ideas to make companies more democratic. These include an actively enforced democratic constitution, guaranteeing basic rights like freedom of speech. He also wants to support new companies and products by providing sources of credit, extensive training programs, and support organizations.[2] Democracy theorists may develop these ideas further in response to economic problems.

❝ This proposal for workers to collectively become their own board of directors also democratizes the enterprise ... Such economic democracy inside enterprises is not only a necessary crisis response; it also fosters real democracy across society as workers will demand similar democracy in the communities where they live. ❞

Richard Wolff, *Capitalism Hits the Fan*

If followed, this proposal could change how corporations manage their operations. If corporations were run more democratically, it would be harder to give large bonuses to executives while some employees struggle financially. Mass layoffs would become harder to justify.

Future Directions

Scholars could further develop Dahl's ideas about corporate democracy. Although Richard D. Wolff,* an American economist and former professor, does not mention Dahl or *Democracy and Its Critics*, his views overlap with Dahl's: both argued that businesses should adopt democratic forms of governance. Wolff suggested there might not be a repeat of the global economic recession if workers "collectively become their own board of directors." The majority of workers would get the power to decide "what is produced, how and where it is produced, and what is done with the proceeds." Wolff argued that this would expand democracy because workers would demand more democracy where they live.[3]

Summary

Dahl has been one of the most influential democratic theorists in the world[4] from the early 1950s. His importance as a theorist is closely linked to the importance of *Democracy and Its Critics*, since the book collected and built on Dahl's entire body of work on democratic theory.

In his various books, Dahl examined real, existing democracies in the modern world. He labeled them polyarchies,* and suggested they fall short of democratic ideals. In *Democracy and Its Critics*, Dahl proposed certain standards that should be met if a country is to be considered a polyarchy, and a separate set of standards for a political process to be considered democratic. He then suggested ways that modern countries might close the gap between polyarchy and democracy.

The importance and success of *Democracy and Its Critics* comes from its broad scope, its richly detailed discussion of theory, and its imaginative conclusions. Dahl wanted to offer an interpretation of democratic theory and practice that would be relevant to the contemporary world.[5] This required him to respond to the problems identified by the critics of democracy, which he did in *Democracy and Its Critics*. Building on this, he outlined the future directions that democracy should take. Dahl skillfully moved between examining the origins of democracy and considering practical and philosophical issues in the democracies of today. His mastery of these topics has made *Democracy and Its Critics* a modern classic.

NOTES

1   Robert A. Dahl, *Democracy and Its Critics* (New Haven, CT: Yale University Press, 1989), 328.

2   Dahl, *Democracy and Its Critics*, 332.

3   Richard D. Wolff, "Capitalism Hits the Fan," *Journal of Psychohistory* 37, no. 2 (2009): 128.

4   See Margaret Levi, "A Conversation with Robert A. Dahl," *Annual Review of Political Science* 12 (2009): 1–9.

5   Dahl, *Democracy and Its Critics*, 2.

GLOSSARY

GLOSSARY OF TERMS

Aggregative democracy: a view that democratic legitimacy is founded in the aggregation (collection and counting) of preferences expressed through voting; it is useful to compare it to "deliberative" democracy.

American Revolution: a period between 1765 and 1783 when colonists in the 13 American Colonies revolted against the British monarchy and founded the United States of America.

Anarchism: a philosophical theory that holds that states should be eliminated and replaced with voluntary associations. Anarchists believe that since states force people to do things they otherwise would not do, they are evil by nature, even those states governed democratically.

APSA (American Political Science Association): a professional organization for students and scholars of political science, founded in 1903.

Aristocracy: the Greek philosopher Aristotle defined this system as rule by a group of the best people. Its more common usage, however, refers to the holding of political authority by a small, usually hereditary, group.

Behavioralism: an approach in political science that saw a surge in importance between 1951 and 1961. Behavioralists studied political behavior associated with elements of American democracy, including voting, public opinion, legislative behavior, and nongovernmental associations and interest groups.

Berlin Wall: a barrier that divided the German city of Berlin from 1961 to 1989. Used to prevent East Germans from leaving their country for the capitalist West, it was a symbol of the conflict between social systems. The fall of the Berlin Wall is commonly regarded as the beginning of the end of European communism.

Capitalism: an economic system where most trade and industry is owned by private firms seeking to generate a profit. Private property, wage labor, investment for profit, and competition are typical features of capitalist economies. The largest examples of capitalist economies are the United States, Europe, and the eastern edge of Asia.

Cold War (1946–89): a period of tension between the Western bloc (America and its allies) and the Eastern bloc (the Soviet Union and its allies). While the US and Soviet Union never engaged in direct military conflict, they engaged in covert and proxy wars and espionage against one another.

Communism: a political system—for example, the regimes established in the Soviet Union in 1922, in Central and Eastern Europe after 1945, and in China in 1949—in which productive property is nationalized and placed under strict government control.

Comparative politics: a field of political science where different political phenomena are analyzed to identify patterns of similarity or difference.

Criterion of enlightened understanding: belief that each citizen should be given adequate and equal opportunities to discover and decide—in the time permitted by the need to decide an issue—the choice that would best serve that citizen's interests.

Deliberative democracy: a view that informed deliberation, not just voting, is essential to democratic legitimacy. Compare with aggregative democracy.

Democracy: while the Greek philosopher Aristotle defined democracy as the chaotic rule by a mob, the modern definition refers to making political decisions by majority vote, and living under the rule of law. "Demos" is Greek for "people" and "kratis" for "power."

Democratic procedures: Dahl said democratic procedures include providing essential rights, avoiding tyranny, promoting freedom and moral independence, and, most importantly, promoting political equality.

Demos: an ancient Greek term that refers to the populace of a city, state, or country. In modern speech, this refers to the common people.

Eastern Bloc: a grouping of communist states in Eastern Europe that lasted between 1947 and 1991.

Elitism: the belief that some quality, such as wealth, intellect, or ancestry, makes some people more important than others.

Enlightenment: an early modern (seventeenth to eighteenth century) cultural, intellectual, and philosophical movement that emphasized social and personal progress through education, science, individualism, and reason.

Equal consideration of interests: the belief that the interests of every person who is subject to a decision must be accurately interpreted and made known during the process of political decision-making.

Equal intrinsic worth: the belief that all people are fundamentally equal by nature and therefore are worthy of equal consideration.

French Revolution (1789): an uprising that overthrew the Bourbon monarchy and established France as a Republic under the slogan Liberty, Equality and Fraternity.

Global economic recession: also known as the Great Recession, this is a period beginning in 2007–8 when production, wages, and living standards in most advanced capitalist countries fell, then suffered from slow growth for a number of years.

Guardianship: the idea that ordinary people are not qualified to govern themselves, and that authority should therefore be handed over to a minority of people whose exceptional qualities of knowledge and virtue qualify them to rule.

Iraq War (2003–11): an armed conflict between the United States and Iraq. After toppling the government of the dictator Saddam Hussein in 2003, the conflict descended into a sectarian civil war, which pitted Iraq's Shi'a and Sunni populations against each other. In December 2011, American forces withdrew from Iraq.

Lippmann–Dewey debate: an exchange of views about the role of citizens in a democracy between two American political theorists, Walter Lippmann and John Dewey. In a series of articles and books in the 1920s, Lippmann argued that citizens could not be sufficiently well informed to run a country, while Dewey was more optimistic.

Logic of political equality: the belief among a group of people that each member is equally well qualified to participate in decision-making.

Longshore worker: people employed to load and unload maritime trade cargo.

MDP societies: Dahl's notion of modern, dynamic, pluralist (MDP) societies. These societies tend to have a relatively high level of income and wealth per capita, a high level of urbanization, great occupational diversity, extensive literacy, a small agricultural population, and an economic order where production is mainly carried out by self-directed firms oriented toward national and international markets.

Minipopulus (minipopuli): a deliberative body (bodies) of randomly selected citizens, whose debates help inform the work of legislatures.

Occupy movement: an international protest movement that began staging demonstrations around the world in 2011, and that shares a commitment to participatory democracy and to combating social and economic inequality.

Oligarchy: an ancient Greek term used to describe a form of government that is dominated by a small group of powerful individuals. The term means rule of the few.

Pluralism: recognizes and values diversity in a political body or group. It is associated with deliberation and equality, rather than instruction.

Polity: a system defined by the Greek philosopher Aristotle as the "good" version of democracy, where the people are managed by the competing interests of a wealthy few. Its common sense definition refers to the form of a government constitution.

Polyarchy: a concept first introduced by Dahl and Charles E. Lindblom in *Politics, Economics, and Welfare* (1953) that means the rule of the many and is contrasted with oligarchy, rule of the few.

Populism: a set of beliefs intended to appeal to the masses of people.

Presidential primaries: every four years the United States holds presidential primary elections to determine the leading candidates for each political party.

Presumption of personal autonomy: a notion that each adult person should have the right to judge whether a policy is in his or her best interest.

Proceduralism: a view of democracy holding that fair procedures, not moral considerations, lead to democratic legitimacy.

Recession: a stage in the business cycle (boom and bust) where economic growth is down, production is down, and unemployment is up.

Representative government: a system of government in which elected delegates represent a group of people.

Republican: a system of government in which the people must participate in ruling, and where people are governed by the rule of law, rather than by a monarch or tyrant.

Soviet Union, or USSR: a kind of "super state" that existed from 1922 to 1991, centered primarily on Russia and its neighbors in Eastern Europe and the northern half of Asia. It was the communist pole of the Cold War, with the United States as its main "rival."

Strong principle of equality: the belief that every adult member of an association is sufficiently well qualified to participate in making binding collective decisions that affect his or her interests.

Suffrage: the right to vote.

Theory: a statement of the relationship between two observations (for example: the theory of gravity explains why an apple, when dropped, will fall).

PEOPLE MENTIONED IN THE TEXT

Bruce Ackerman (b. 1943) is an American constitutional law scholar and political scientist whose work has been influential in constitutional law, political philosophy, and public policy.

Aristotle (384–322 B.C.E.) was a Greek philosopher and founding figure of Western philosophy. Writing extensively on ethics, politics, aesthetics, logic, metaphysics, and science, he is famous for his analysis of the different forms of governance.

George W. Bush (b. 1946) was the 43rd president of the United States, in office from 2001 to 2009.

Elizabeth Cohen (b. 1973) is a political scientist specializing in immigration and citizenship.

Joshua Cohen (b. 1951) is an American political theorist trained in political philosophy, best known for his work on deliberative democracy.

Cary Coglianese is a law scholar and political scientist specializing in regulation and regulatory processes.

Michael Coppedge is an American political scientist specializing in democracy theory, party systems, and elections in Latin America.

John Dewey (1859–1952) was an American philosopher and psychologist. He is best known for his work on pragmatism.

John Dryzek (b. 1953) is a British-born social and political theorist, best known for his work on deliberative democracy.

Jean Bethke Elshtain (1941–2013) was an American political philosopher and well-known public intellectual whose scholarship focused on the relationship between politics and ethics.

James Fishkin (b. 1948) is a scholar of communication, best known for his work on deliberative democracy.

Robert Goodin (b. 1950) is an American-born political philosopher and political scientist whose work focuses on political theory and public policy.

Amy Gutmann (b. 1949) is an American political scientist and president of the University of Pennsylvania. She is best known for her work on democratic theory in her book, *Democratic Education* (1987).

Samuel Huntington (1927–2008) was a professor of international relations at Harvard University from 1963 until his death. His book *The Clash of Civilizations and the Remaking of World Order* (1996), is widely considered the most influential post-Cold War analysis of international order.

Terry Lynn Karl is a political scientist specializing in comparative politics and international relations, with a particular focus on democratic transitions, human rights and the politics of oil-exporting countries.

Charles E. Lindblom (b. 1917) is an American political scientist and economist who was part of the pluralist school of thought, which dominated American political science from the late 1950s until the early 1960s.

Walter Lippman (1889–1974) was an American journalist and political commentator, who gained international recognition for coining the term "Cold War" to describe American–Soviet relations following World War II. He is also noted for his work on democratic theory in his book, *Public Opinion* (1922).

John Locke (1632–1704) was an English philosopher and physician, known for being an Enlightenment thinker and for his ideas about the political philosophy known as liberalism.

James Madison (1751–1836) was the fourth president of the United States, and played a central role in the drafting of the US Constitution and the Bill of Rights. He is also famous for his lengthy public debate about the nature of American democracy with Alexander Hamilton and John Jay, which was captured in the *Federalist Papers* (1788).

Jack Nagel is an American political scientist who specializes in democratic theory, elections, and voting theory.

Thomas Paine (1736/7–1809) was a British American political thinker and social reformer. His *Common Sense* pamphlet was widely credited with helping inspire the shape of the American Revolution.

Plato (428/7–348/7 B.C.E.) was a Greek philosopher who founded the Academy in Athens, the first Western institution of higher learning.

Wolfgang H. Reinicke is a public policy scholar specializing in global governance, global finance, and international economic institutions.

Melvin Rogers is an associate professor of political science at Emery University. His work focuses primarily on the contributions John Dewey made to the study of democracy.

Jean-Jacques Rousseau (1712–78) was a Genevan philosopher, famous for his works about liberty and citizenship.

Philippe Schmitter (b. 1936) is a political scientist best known for his work on democratization and transitions from authoritarian rule.

Joseph Schumpeter (1883–1950) was an Austrian American political scientist known for his contribution to democratic theory and for arguing that "rule by the people" was undesirable.

Abdel-Fattah el-Sisi (b. 1954): is the current president of Egypt, who ousted former president Mohammad Morsi in 2013. He was re-elected with 93 percent of the vote in 2014.

Socrates (c. 469–399 B.C.E.) was a Greek philosopher and founding figure of Western philosophy. He is best known for his work on ethics and epistemology (the theory of knowledge).

Dennis Thompson (b. 1940) is a professor of political science at Harvard University, known for his work on political ethics and democratic theory in his text, *The Democratic Citizen* (1970).

Henry David Thoreau (1817–62) was an American essayist and poet, best known for his essay *Civil Disobedience* (1849), which influenced the policy of passive resistance promoted by Mahatma Gandhi (1869–1948).

Alexis de Tocqueville (1805–59) was a French aristocrat and political thinker. He is best known for his work on American democracy.

Richard D. Wolff (b. 1942) is an American economist best known for adopting a new approach to political economy associated with Marxian economics. He has also published works focusing on the global capitalist crisis.

WORKS CITED

WORKS CITED

Ackerman, Bruce A., and James S. Fishkin. *Deliberation Day*. New Haven, CT: Yale University Press, 2004.

Coglianese, Cary. "Review of *Democracy and Its Critics* by Robert A. Dahl." *Michigan Law Review* 88 (1990): 1662–7.

"Weak Democracy, Strong Information: The Role of Information Technology in the Rulemaking Process." Public Law Working Paper, No. 07-04. 2007.

Cohen, Elizabeth F. *Semi-citizenship in Democratic Politics*. Cambridge: Cambridge University Press, 2009.

Cohen, Joshua. "Deliberation and Democratic Legitimacy." In *Deliberative Democracy: Essays on Reason and Politics*, edited by James Bohman and William Rehg, 67–92. Cambridge, MA: The MIT Press, 1997.

"Democracy and Liberty." In *Deliberative Democracy*, edited by Jon Elster, 185–231. New York: Cambridge University Press, 1998.

"Institutional Argument ... Is Diminished by the Limited Examination of the Issues of Principle." *The Journal of Politics* 53, no. 1 (1991): 221–5.

"Procedure and Substance in Deliberative Democracy." In *Democracy and Difference: Contesting the Boundaries of the Political*, edited by Seyla Benhabib, 95–119. Princeton, NJ: Princeton University Press, 1996.

Cohen, Joshua, and Joel Rogers. *On Democracy: Toward a Transformation of American Society*. New York: Penguin Books, 1983.

Coppedge, Michael, and Wolfgang H. Reinicke. "Measuring Polyarchy." *Studies in Comparative International Development* 25, no. 1 (1990): 51–72.

Dahl, Robert A. *Democracy and Its Critics*. New Haven, CT: Yale University Press, 1989.

On Political Equality. New Haven, CT: Yale University Press, 2006.

Polyarchy: Participation and Opposition. New Haven, CT: Yale University Press, 1971.

A Preface to Democratic Theory. Chicago: University of Chicago Press, 1956.

"A Rejoinder." *The Journal of Politics* 53, no. 1 (1991): 226–31.

Who Governs? Democracy and Power in an American City. New Haven, CT: Yale University Press, 1961.

Dahl, Robert A., and Margaret Levi. "A Conversation with Robert A. Dahl." *Annual Review of Political Science* 12 (2009): 1–9.

Elshtain, Jean Bethke. "If Things Are, on the Whole, so Good, Whence the Widespread Perception of Decay and Decline?" *The Journal of Politics* 53, no. 1 (1991): 218–21.

Fishkin, James S. *Democracy and Deliberation: New Directions for Democratic Reform*. New Haven, CT: Yale University Press, 1991.

Goodin, Robert E., and John S. Dryzek. "Deliberative Impacts: The Macro-Political Uptake of Mini-Publics." *Politics and Society* 34, no. 2 (2006): 219–44.

"Making use of mini-publics." In *Innovating Democracy: Democratic Theory and Practice after the Deliberative Turn*, edited by Robert E. Goodin, 11–37. Oxford: Oxford University Press, 2008.

Hurley, Susan L. *Natural Reasons: Personality and Polity*. Oxford: Oxford University Press, 1992.

Manley, John F. "Neo-Pluralism: A Class Analysis of Pluralism I and Pluralism II." *The American Political Science Review* 77, no. 2 (1983): 368–83.

Munck, Gerardo L. *Measuring Democracy: A Bridge Between Scholarship and Politics* (Baltimore, MD: Johns Hopkins University Press, 2009).

Nagel, Jack H. "A Democrat First and Foremost, Rather than a Liberal in the Strict Sense." *The Journal of Politics* 53, no. 1 (1991): 215–18.

Pennock, J. Roland. "Review." *Political Theory* 18, no. 3 (1990): 512–18.

Pye, Lucian W. "Book Reviews: Political Theory." *American Political Science Review* 84, no. 2 (1990): 627–29.

Schmitter, Philippe C., and Terry Lynn Karl. "What democracy is … and is not." *Journal of Democracy* 2, no. 3 (1991): 75–88.

Van Evera, Stephen. "Primed for Peace: Europe after the Cold War." *International Security* 15, no. 3 (1990/91): 7–57.

Wolff, Richard D. "Capitalism Hits the Fan." *Journal of Psychohistory* 37, no. 2 (2009): 128.

THE MACAT LIBRARY
BY DISCIPLINE

The Macat Library By Discipline

AFRICANA STUDIES

Chinua Achebe's *An Image of Africa: Racism in Conrad's Heart of Darkness*
W. E. B. Du Bois's *The Souls of Black Folk*
Zora Neale Huston's *Characteristics of Negro Expression*
Martin Luther King Jr's *Why We Can't Wait*
Toni Morrison's *Playing in the Dark: Whiteness in the American Literary Imagination*

ANTHROPOLOGY

Arjun Appadurai's *Modernity at Large: Cultural Dimensions of Globalisation*
Philippe Ariès's *Centuries of Childhood*
Franz Boas's *Race, Language and Culture*
Kim Chan & Renée Mauborgne's *Blue Ocean Strategy*
Jared Diamond's *Guns, Germs & Steel: the Fate of Human Societies*
Jared Diamond's *Collapse: How Societies Choose to Fail or Survive*
E. E. Evans-Pritchard's *Witchcraft, Oracles and Magic Among the Azande*
James Ferguson's *The Anti-Politics Machine*
Clifford Geertz's *The Interpretation of Cultures*
David Graeber's *Debt: the First 5000 Years*
Karen Ho's *Liquidated: An Ethnography of Wall Street*
Geert Hofstede's *Culture's Consequences: Comparing Values, Behaviors, Institutes and Organizations across Nations*
Claude Lévi-Strauss's *Structural Anthropology*
Jay Macleod's *Ain't No Makin' It: Aspirations and Attainment in a Low-Income Neighborhood*
Saba Mahmood's *The Politics of Piety: The Islamic Revival and the Feminist Subject*
Marcel Mauss's *The Gift*

BUSINESS

Jean Lave & Etienne Wenger's *Situated Learning*
Theodore Levitt's *Marketing Myopia*
Burton G. Malkiel's *A Random Walk Down Wall Street*
Douglas McGregor's *The Human Side of Enterprise*
Michael Porter's *Competitive Strategy: Creating and Sustaining Superior Performance*
John Kotter's *Leading Change*
C. K. Prahalad & Gary Hamel's *The Core Competence of the Corporation*

CRIMINOLOGY

Michelle Alexander's *The New Jim Crow: Mass Incarceration in the Age of Colorblindness*
Michael R. Gottfredson & Travis Hirschi's *A General Theory of Crime*
Richard Herrnstein & Charles A. Murray's *The Bell Curve: Intelligence and Class Structure in American Life*
Elizabeth Loftus's *Eyewitness Testimony*
Jay Macleod's *Ain't No Makin' It: Aspirations and Attainment in a Low-Income Neighborhood*
Philip Zimbardo's *The Lucifer Effect*

ECONOMICS

Janet Abu-Lughod's *Before European Hegemony*
Ha-Joon Chang's *Kicking Away the Ladder*
David Brion Davis's *The Problem of Slavery in the Age of Revolution*
Milton Friedman's *The Role of Monetary Policy*
Milton Friedman's *Capitalism and Freedom*
David Graeber's *Debt: the First 5000 Years*
Friedrich Hayek's *The Road to Serfdom*
Karen Ho's *Liquidated: An Ethnography of Wall Street*

John Maynard Keynes's *The General Theory of Employment, Interest and Money*
Charles P. Kindleberger's *Manias, Panics and Crashes*
Robert Lucas's *Why Doesn't Capital Flow from Rich to Poor Countries?*
Burton G. Malkiel's *A Random Walk Down Wall Street*
Thomas Robert Malthus's *An Essay on the Principle of Population*
Karl Marx's *Capital*
Thomas Piketty's *Capital in the Twenty-First Century*
Amartya Sen's *Development as Freedom*
Adam Smith's *The Wealth of Nations*
Nassim Nicholas Taleb's *The Black Swan: The Impact of the Highly Improbable*
Amos Tversky's & Daniel Kahneman's *Judgment under Uncertainty: Heuristics and Biases*
Mahbub Ul Haq's *Reflections on Human Development*
Max Weber's *The Protestant Ethic and the Spirit of Capitalism*

FEMINISM AND GENDER STUDIES

Judith Butler's *Gender Trouble*
Simone De Beauvoir's *The Second Sex*
Michel Foucault's *History of Sexuality*
Betty Friedan's *The Feminine Mystique*
Saba Mahmood's *The Politics of Piety: The Islamic Revival and the Feminist Subject*
Joan Wallach Scott's *Gender and the Politics of History*
Mary Wollstonecraft's *A Vindication of the Rights of Woman*
Virginia Woolf's *A Room of One's Own*

GEOGRAPHY

The Brundtland Report's *Our Common Future*
Rachel Carson's *Silent Spring*
Charles Darwin's *On the Origin of Species*
James Ferguson's *The Anti-Politics Machine*
Jane Jacobs's *The Death and Life of Great American Cities*
James Lovelock's *Gaia: A New Look at Life on Earth*
Amartya Sen's *Development as Freedom*
Mathis Wackernagel & William Rees's *Our Ecological Footprint*

HISTORY

Janet Abu-Lughod's *Before European Hegemony*
Benedict Anderson's *Imagined Communities*
Bernard Bailyn's *The Ideological Origins of the American Revolution*
Hanna Batatu's *The Old Social Classes And The Revolutionary Movements Of Iraq*
Christopher Browning's *Ordinary Men: Reserve Police Batallion 101 and the Final Solution in Poland*
Edmund Burke's *Reflections on the Revolution in France*
William Cronon's *Nature's Metropolis: Chicago And The Great West*
Alfred W. Crosby's *The Columbian Exchange*
Hamid Dabashi's *Iran: A People Interrupted*
David Brion Davis's *The Problem of Slavery in the Age of Revolution*
Nathalie Zemon Davis's *The Return of Martin Guerre*
Jared Diamond's *Guns, Germs & Steel: the Fate of Human Societies*
Frank Dikotter's *Mao's Great Famine*
John W Dower's *War Without Mercy: Race And Power In The Pacific War*
W. E. B. Du Bois's *The Souls of Black Folk*
Richard J. Evans's *In Defence of History*
Lucien Febvre's *The Problem of Unbelief in the 16th Century*
Sheila Fitzpatrick's *Everyday Stalinism*

The Macat Library By Discipline

Eric Foner's *Reconstruction: America's Unfinished Revolution, 1863-1877*
Michel Foucault's *Discipline and Punish*
Michel Foucault's *History of Sexuality*
Francis Fukuyama's *The End of History and the Last Man*
John Lewis Gaddis's *We Now Know: Rethinking Cold War History*
Ernest Gellner's *Nations and Nationalism*
Eugene Genovese's *Roll, Jordan, Roll: The World the Slaves Made*
Carlo Ginzburg's *The Night Battles*
Daniel Goldhagen's *Hitler's Willing Executioners*
Jack Goldstone's *Revolution and Rebellion in the Early Modern World*
Antonio Gramsci's *The Prison Notebooks*
Alexander Hamilton, John Jay & James Madison's *The Federalist Papers*
Christopher Hill's *The World Turned Upside Down*
Carole Hillenbrand's *The Crusades: Islamic Perspectives*
Thomas Hobbes's *Leviathan*
Eric Hobsbawm's *The Age Of Revolution*
John A. Hobson's *Imperialism: A Study*
Albert Hourani's *History of the Arab Peoples*
Samuel P. Huntington's *The Clash of Civilizations and the Remaking of World Order*
C. L. R. James's *The Black Jacobins*
Tony Judt's *Postwar: A History of Europe Since 1945*
Ernst Kantorowicz's *The King's Two Bodies: A Study in Medieval Political Theology*
Paul Kennedy's *The Rise and Fall of the Great Powers*
Ian Kershaw's *The "Hitler Myth": Image and Reality in the Third Reich*
John Maynard Keynes's *The General Theory of Employment, Interest and Money*
Charles P. Kindleberger's *Manias, Panics and Crashes*
Martin Luther King Jr's *Why We Can't Wait*
Henry Kissinger's *World Order: Reflections on the Character of Nations and the Course of History*
Thomas Kuhn's *The Structure of Scientific Revolutions*
Georges Lefebvre's *The Coming of the French Revolution*
John Locke's *Two Treatises of Government*
Niccolò Machiavelli's *The Prince*
Thomas Robert Malthus's *An Essay on the Principle of Population*
Mahmood Mamdani's *Citizen and Subject: Contemporary Africa And The Legacy Of Late Colonialism*
Karl Marx's *Capital*
Stanley Milgram's *Obedience to Authority*
John Stuart Mill's *On Liberty*
Thomas Paine's *Common Sense*
Thomas Paine's *Rights of Man*
Geoffrey Parker's *Global Crisis: War, Climate Change and Catastrophe in the Seventeenth Century*
Jonathan Riley-Smith's *The First Crusade and the Idea of Crusading*
Jean-Jacques Rousseau's *The Social Contract*
Joan Wallach Scott's *Gender and the Politics of History*
Theda Skocpol's *States and Social Revolutions*
Adam Smith's *The Wealth of Nations*
Timothy Snyder's *Bloodlands: Europe Between Hitler and Stalin*
Sun Tzu's *The Art of War*
Keith Thomas's *Religion and the Decline of Magic*
Thucydides's *The History of the Peloponnesian War*
Frederick Jackson Turner's *The Significance of the Frontier in American History*
Odd Arne Westad's *The Global Cold War: Third World Interventions And The Making Of Our Times*

LITERATURE

Chinua Achebe's *An Image of Africa: Racism in Conrad's Heart of Darkness*
Roland Barthes's *Mythologies*
Homi K. Bhabha's *The Location of Culture*
Judith Butler's *Gender Trouble*
Simone De Beauvoir's *The Second Sex*
Ferdinand De Saussure's *Course in General Linguistics*
T. S. Eliot's *The Sacred Wood: Essays on Poetry and Criticism*
Zora Neale Huston's *Characteristics of Negro Expression*
Toni Morrison's *Playing in the Dark: Whiteness in the American Literary Imagination*
Edward Said's *Orientalism*
Gayatri Chakravorty Spivak's *Can the Subaltern Speak?*
Mary Wollstonecraft's *A Vindication of the Rights of Women*
Virginia Woolf's *A Room of One's Own*

PHILOSOPHY

Elizabeth Anscombe's *Modern Moral Philosophy*
Hannah Arendt's *The Human Condition*
Aristotle's *Metaphysics*
Aristotle's *Nicomachean Ethics*
Edmund Gettier's *Is Justified True Belief Knowledge?*
Georg Wilhelm Friedrich Hegel's *Phenomenology of Spirit*
David Hume's *Dialogues Concerning Natural Religion*
David Hume's *The Enquiry for Human Understanding*
Immanuel Kant's *Religion within the Boundaries of Mere Reason*
Immanuel Kant's *Critique of Pure Reason*
Søren Kierkegaard's *The Sickness Unto Death*
Søren Kierkegaard's *Fear and Trembling*
C. S. Lewis's *The Abolition of Man*
Alasdair MacIntyre's *After Virtue*
Marcus Aurelius's *Meditations*
Friedrich Nietzsche's *On the Genealogy of Morality*
Friedrich Nietzsche's *Beyond Good and Evil*
Plato's *Republic*
Plato's *Symposium*
Jean-Jacques Rousseau's *The Social Contract*
Gilbert Ryle's *The Concept of Mind*
Baruch Spinoza's *Ethics*
Sun Tzu's *The Art of War*
Ludwig Wittgenstein's *Philosophical Investigations*

POLITICS

Benedict Anderson's *Imagined Communities*
Aristotle's *Politics*
Bernard Bailyn's *The Ideological Origins of the American Revolution*
Edmund Burke's *Reflections on the Revolution in France*
John C. Calhoun's *A Disquisition on Government*
Ha-Joon Chang's *Kicking Away the Ladder*
Hamid Dabashi's *Iran: A People Interrupted*
Hamid Dabashi's *Theology of Discontent: The Ideological Foundation of the Islamic Revolution in Iran*
Robert Dahl's *Democracy and its Critics*
Robert Dahl's *Who Governs?*
David Brion Davis's *The Problem of Slavery in the Age of Revolution*

The Macat Library By Discipline

Alexis De Tocqueville's *Democracy in America*
James Ferguson's *The Anti-Politics Machine*
Frank Dikotter's *Mao's Great Famine*
Sheila Fitzpatrick's *Everyday Stalinism*
Eric Foner's *Reconstruction: America's Unfinished Revolution, 1863-1877*
Milton Friedman's *Capitalism and Freedom*
Francis Fukuyama's *The End of History and the Last Man*
John Lewis Gaddis's *We Now Know: Rethinking Cold War History*
Ernest Gellner's *Nations and Nationalism*
David Graeber's *Debt: the First 5000 Years*
Antonio Gramsci's *The Prison Notebooks*
Alexander Hamilton, John Jay & James Madison's *The Federalist Papers*
Friedrich Hayek's *The Road to Serfdom*
Christopher Hill's *The World Turned Upside Down*
Thomas Hobbes's *Leviathan*
John A. Hobson's *Imperialism: A Study*
Samuel P. Huntington's *The Clash of Civilizations and the Remaking of World Order*
Tony Judt's *Postwar: A History of Europe Since 1945*
David C. Kang's *China Rising: Peace, Power and Order in East Asia*
Paul Kennedy's *The Rise and Fall of Great Powers*
Robert Keohane's *After Hegemony*
Martin Luther King Jr.'s *Why We Can't Wait*
Henry Kissinger's *World Order: Reflections on the Character of Nations and the Course of History*
John Locke's *Two Treatises of Government*
Niccolò Machiavelli's *The Prince*
Thomas Robert Malthus's *An Essay on the Principle of Population*
Mahmood Mamdani's *Citizen and Subject: Contemporary Africa And The Legacy Of Late Colonialism*
Karl Marx's *Capital*
John Stuart Mill's *On Liberty*
John Stuart Mill's *Utilitarianism*
Hans Morgenthau's *Politics Among Nations*
Thomas Paine's *Common Sense*
Thomas Paine's *Rights of Man*
Thomas Piketty's *Capital in the Twenty-First Century*
Robert D. Putman's *Bowling Alone*
John Rawls's *Theory of Justice*
Jean-Jacques Rousseau's *The Social Contract*
Theda Skocpol's *States and Social Revolutions*
Adam Smith's *The Wealth of Nations*
Sun Tzu's *The Art of War*
Henry David Thoreau's *Civil Disobedience*
Thucydides's *The History of the Peloponnesian War*
Kenneth Waltz's *Theory of International Politics*
Max Weber's *Politics as a Vocation*
Odd Arne Westad's *The Global Cold War: Third World Interventions And The Making Of Our Times*

POSTCOLONIAL STUDIES

Roland Barthes's *Mythologies*
Frantz Fanon's *Black Skin, White Masks*
Homi K. Bhabha's *The Location of Culture*
Gustavo Gutiérrez's *A Theology of Liberation*
Edward Said's *Orientalism*
Gayatri Chakravorty Spivak's *Can the Subaltern Speak?*

PSYCHOLOGY

Gordon Allport's *The Nature of Prejudice*
Alan Baddeley & Graham Hitch's *Aggression: A Social Learning Analysis*
Albert Bandura's *Aggression: A Social Learning Analysis*
Leon Festinger's *A Theory of Cognitive Dissonance*
Sigmund Freud's *The Interpretation of Dreams*
Betty Friedan's *The Feminine Mystique*
Michael R. Gottfredson & Travis Hirschi's *A General Theory of Crime*
Eric Hoffer's *The True Believer: Thoughts on the Nature of Mass Movements*
William James's *Principles of Psychology*
Elizabeth Loftus's *Eyewitness Testimony*
A. H. Maslow's *A Theory of Human Motivation*
Stanley Milgram's *Obedience to Authority*
Steven Pinker's *The Better Angels of Our Nature*
Oliver Sacks's *The Man Who Mistook His Wife For a Hat*
Richard Thaler & Cass Sunstein's *Nudge: Improving Decisions About Health, Wealth and Happiness*
Amos Tversky's *Judgment under Uncertainty: Heuristics and Biases*
Philip Zimbardo's *The Lucifer Effect*

SCIENCE

Rachel Carson's *Silent Spring*
William Cronon's *Nature's Metropolis: Chicago And The Great West*
Alfred W. Crosby's *The Columbian Exchange*
Charles Darwin's *On the Origin of Species*
Richard Dawkin's *The Selfish Gene*
Thomas Kuhn's *The Structure of Scientific Revolutions*
Geoffrey Parker's *Global Crisis: War, Climate Change and Catastrophe in the Seventeenth Century*
Mathis Wackernagel & William Rees's *Our Ecological Footprint*

SOCIOLOGY

Michelle Alexander's *The New Jim Crow: Mass Incarceration in the Age of Colorblindness*
Gordon Allport's *The Nature of Prejudice*
Albert Bandura's *Aggression: A Social Learning Analysis*
Hanna Batatu's *The Old Social Classes And The Revolutionary Movements Of Iraq*
Ha-Joon Chang's *Kicking Away the Ladder*
W. E. B. Du Bois's *The Souls of Black Folk*
Émile Durkheim's *On Suicide*
Frantz Fanon's *Black Skin, White Masks*
Frantz Fanon's *The Wretched of the Earth*
Eric Foner's *Reconstruction: America's Unfinished Revolution, 1863-1877*
Eugene Genovese's *Roll, Jordan, Roll: The World the Slaves Made*
Jack Goldstone's *Revolution and Rebellion in the Early Modern World*
Antonio Gramsci's *The Prison Notebooks*
Richard Herrnstein & Charles A Murray's *The Bell Curve: Intelligence and Class Structure in American Life*
Eric Hoffer's *The True Believer: Thoughts on the Nature of Mass Movements*
Jane Jacobs's *The Death and Life of Great American Cities*
Robert Lucas's *Why Doesn't Capital Flow from Rich to Poor Countries?*
Jay Macleod's *Ain't No Makin' It: Aspirations and Attainment in a Low Income Neighborhood*
Elaine May's *Homeward Bound: American Families in the Cold War Era*
Douglas McGregor's *The Human Side of Enterprise*
C. Wright Mills's *The Sociological Imagination*

The Macat Library By Discipline

Thomas Piketty's *Capital in the Twenty-First Century*
Robert D. Putman's *Bowling Alone*
David Riesman's *The Lonely Crowd: A Study of the Changing American Character*
Edward Said's *Orientalism*
Joan Wallach Scott's *Gender and the Politics of History*
Theda Skocpol's *States and Social Revolutions*
Max Weber's *The Protestant Ethic and the Spirit of Capitalism*

THEOLOGY

Augustine's *Confessions*
Benedict's *Rule of St Benedict*
Gustavo Gutiérrez's *A Theology of Liberation*
Carole Hillenbrand's *The Crusades: Islamic Perspectives*
David Hume's *Dialogues Concerning Natural Religion*
Immanuel Kant's *Religion within the Boundaries of Mere Reason*
Ernst Kantorowicz's *The King's Two Bodies: A Study in Medieval Political Theology*
Søren Kierkegaard's *The Sickness Unto Death*
C. S. Lewis's *The Abolition of Man*
Saba Mahmood's *The Politics of Piety: The Islamic Revival and the Feminist Subject*
Baruch Spinoza's *Ethics*
Keith Thomas's *Religion and the Decline of Magic*

COMING SOON

Chris Argyris's *The Individual and the Organisation*
Seyla Benhabib's *The Rights of Others*
Walter Benjamin's *The Work Of Art in the Age of Mechanical Reproduction*
John Berger's *Ways of Seeing*
Pierre Bourdieu's *Outline of a Theory of Practice*
Mary Douglas's *Purity and Danger*
Roland Dworkin's *Taking Rights Seriously*
James G. March's *Exploration and Exploitation in Organisational Learning*
Ikujiro Nonaka's *A Dynamic Theory of Organizational Knowledge Creation*
Griselda Pollock's *Vision and Difference*
Amartya Sen's *Inequality Re-Examined*
Susan Sontag's *On Photography*
Yasser Tabbaa's *The Transformation of Islamic Art*
Ludwig von Mises's *Theory of Money and Credit*

Macat Pairs

Analyse historical and modern issues from opposite sides of an argument. Pairs include:

HOW TO RUN AN ECONOMY

John Maynard Keynes's
The General Theory OF Employment, Interest and Money

Classical economics suggests that market economies are self-correcting in times of recession or depression, and tend toward full employment and output. But English economist John Maynard Keynes disagrees.

In his ground-breaking 1936 study *The General Theory*, Keynes argues that traditional economics has misunderstood the causes of unemployment. Employment is not determined by the price of labor; it is directly linked to demand. Keynes believes market economies are by nature unstable, and so require government intervention. Spurred on by the social catastrophe of the Great Depression of the 1930s, he sets out to revolutionize the way the world thinks

Milton Friedman's
The Role of Monetary Policy

Friedman's 1968 paper changed the course of economic theory. In just 17 pages, he demolished existing theory and outlined an effective alternate monetary policy designed to secure 'high employment, stable prices and rapid growth.'

Friedman demonstrated that monetary policy plays a vital role in broader economic stability and argued that economists got their monetary policy wrong in the 1950s and 1960s by misunderstanding the relationship between inflation and unemployment. Previous generations of economists had believed that governments could permanently decrease unemployment by permitting inflation—and vice versa. Friedman's most original contribution was to show that this supposed trade-off is an illusion that only works in the short term.

Macat analyses are available from all good bookshops and libraries.

Access hundreds of analyses through one, multimedia tool.
Join free for one month **library.macat.com**

Macat Disciplines

Access the greatest ideas and thinkers across entire disciplines, including

THE FUTURE OF DEMOCRACY

Robert A. Dahl's, *Democracy and Its Critics*
Robert A. Dahl's, *Who Governs?*
Alexis De Toqueville's, *Democracy in America*
Niccolò Machiavelli's, *The Prince*
John Stuart Mill's, *On Liberty*
Robert D. Putnam's, *Bowling Alone*
Jean-Jacques Rousseau's, *The Social Contract*
Henry David Thoreau's, *Civil Disobedience*

Macat analyses are available from all good bookshops and libraries.

Access hundreds of analyses through one, multimedia tool.
Join free for one month **library.macat.com**

Macat Disciplines

Access the greatest ideas and thinkers across entire disciplines, including

TOTALITARIANISM

Sheila Fitzpatrick's, *Everyday Stalinism*
Ian Kershaw's, *The "Hitler Myth"*
Timothy Snyder's, *Bloodlands*

Printed in the United States
by Baker & Taylor Publisher Services